I0221428

Alexander Meyrowitz

Hebrew Grammar

.

Alexander Meyrowitz

Hebrew Grammar

ISBN/EAN: 9783337316150

Printed in Europe, USA, Canada, Australia, Japan

Cover: Foto ©Paul-Georg Meister /pixelio.de

More available books at **www.hansebooks.com**

תורת לשׁון עברי

HEBREW GRAMMAR

BY

ALEXANDER MEYROWITZ, A.M., Ph.D.

PROFESSOR OF HEBREW AND SHEMITIC LITERATURE IN THE
UNIVERSITY OF THE STATE OF MISSOURI.

PUBLISHED AT THE UNIVERSITY, COLUMBIA, MISSOURI.

NEW YORK:

PRINTED AT INDUSTRIAL SCHOOL, HEBREW ORPHAN ASYLUM,
76TH STREET, NEAR THIRD AVENUE.

1877.

PREFACE.

The number of Hebrew Grammars already published would seem to exceed the scholars studying this language. And yet there are but few which are of real use. Some, like Gesenius, are too large, and are written rather for the scholar than for the student. Others are too meagre to satisfy even the beginner. After having been a teacher of Hebrew for more than thirty years, I believe I have found the middle way. I have omitted the Guttural verbs in my Tables, their deviation being but in the vocalization; but I have added, besides the double anomalous verbs, (e. g. פ"ן and ל"ה) the verbs הָיָה, יֵשׁ, לָקַח, הָלַךְ, etc., as it will be seen by glancing at the Tables. And though this work will not be the last, and critics may find fault with this as I have found with others, I believe nevertheless that it will be of great use to the student, even for self-instruction, and facilitate the comprehension of the Word of God revealed for the salvation of men, which is my greatest aim and desire. There are three systems of pronunciation of the Hebrew, viz., Polish, German, and Portuguese. I follow the Polish, because it is the most common among the Jews.

It gives me pleasure to acknowledge that the appearance of this work before the public is chiefly owing to the munificence of the Rev. S. S. Laws, LL.D., President of the State University of Missouri.

ALEXR. MEYROWITZ.

Columbia, Mo., 28th April, 1877.

§ I.—LETTERS.

———

1. The Hebrew letters in present use are the square Chaldee, derived from the Palmyrene alphabet, adopted by Ezra. The original Hebrew letters are the Phœnician, found on monuments and the Maccabean coins.

2. All the letters are consonants, except א and ע, also ו at the beginning of a word, where they serve to express a vowel syllable, e. g., אַהֲרֹן Aharon, אָדָם Odom, עֲמֹד omod, עָפָר ophor, וּבֵין uvain, וּמָפְּרִי umipri; the vowels are expressed by lines and dots above, below, or within the letters.

N.B.—Hebrew was originally written without vowels, like Arabic and Syriac.

Letters.	Finals.	Number.	Hebrew Pronunciation.	English Pronunciation.	Meaning.
א		1	אָלֶף	Olaph.	An ox.
ב		2	בֵּית	Baith.	A house.
ג		3	גָּמָל	Gamal.	A camel.
ד		4	דָּלֶת	Deleth.	A door.
ה		5	הֵא	Hai.	(Doubtful.)
ו		6	וָו	Vav.	A hook.
ז		7	זַיִן	Zayin.	A weapon.
ח		8	חֵית	Chaith.	A hedge.
ט		9	טֵית	Taith.	A serpent.
י		10	יָד	Yod.	A hand.
כ	ך 500	20	כַּף	Kaph.	A palm, paw.
ל		30	לָמֶד	Lomaid.	A goad.
מ	ם 600	40	מִים	Maim.	Water.
נ	ן 700	50	נוּן	Nun.	A fish.
ס		60	סָמֶךְ	Somech.	A support.
ע		70	עַיִן	Ayin.	An eye.
פ	ף 800	80	פֵּה	Peh.	A mouth.
צ	ץ 900	90	צָדִי	Tsodai.	A fish hook.
ק		100	קוּף	Kuph.	A monkey.
ר		200	רֹאשׁ	Rosh.	A head.
שׁ		300	שֵׁן	Shain.	A tooth.
ת		400	תָּיו	Thav.	A sign, cross.

3. It will be seen in the above table that five letters assume a different form when at the end of a word, wherefore they are called *finals*. They owe their origin to the time when writing was still done without dividing the words, and to mark the end of a word, *final letters* were introduced. When in process of time the words were divided from one another, all the *finals* were dropped except the five, because they served as numerals for 500. 600, etc.

4. The whole alphabet is primarily divided into two parts : *a.* Radicals, *b.* Serviles.

> *a.* **Radicals** are those letters which are used only for the formation of nouns and verbs, consisting chiefly of three letters, which form the *root* of a noun or verb.
>
> *b.* *Serviles* are those letters which, besides being used in the formation of nouns and verbs, are also used as prefixes or suffixes to nouns and verbs, to express other parts of speech. These serviles include half the alphabet, and are :

א, when prefixed to a verb in the future tense, denotes the personal pronoun, nominative 1st singular common.

ב prefixed to any word, denotes the prepositions *in*, *by*, or *with*.

ה with a pathach under it (הַ), when prefixed to a noun with a daghesh (*i. e.*, a point) in its first letter, *e. g.*, הַמֶּלֶךְ [or, if the first letter of the noun is one of the Gutturals, ע, ה, ח, א, which cannot take a daghesh,* the prefixed ה is with komats הָ instead of pathach הַ] it denotes the definite article. ה suffixed to the imperative, denotes the precative, *e. g.*, לְכָה, *age*, come now! ה prefixed to the participle of the verb denotes the relative pron. *who, that*. ה suffixed to the future 1st sing. or pl. com. denotes the future *optative*. ה prefixed to any word with Chatuf Pathach הֲ denotes an *interrogation, e. g.*, הֲשֹׁמֵר whether keeping ? (Gen. iv. 9), הֲמִן whether from ? ה with a Mappik (הּ) suffixed to a noun denotes the posses-

---

* The effect of a Daghesh in the middle of a word is to double the letter, but the Gutturals cannot be doubled.

8

sive pron. 3d pers. fem. sing., *e. g.* זַרְעָהּ her seed (Gen. iii. 15), ה without a Mappik denotes the proposition *to*, *e. g.* סְדֹמָה to Sodom (Gen. xix. 1).

ו at the beginning of any word (except in eleven words, most of them being proper names) denotes the conjunctions: and, but, even, both . . . and.

י prefixed to a verb in the future tense denotes the pers. pron. nom. 3d pers. sing. or plur. Suffixed to a noun it denotes the possessive pron. first. pers. sing. com.

כ prefixed to any word denotes the adverb *like*. ךָ (with a vowel) suffixed to a noun denotes the possessive pron. 2d person masc. sing. Without a vowel, ךְ, poss. pron. 2d pers. fem. singular.

ל prefixed to any word denotes the preposition *to*. Prefixed to the infinitive construct, denotes *in order to*.

מ with a Cheerick under it, prefixed to any word with a Daghesh in its first letter [and if the first letter be a Guttural which cannot take a Daghesh,* the Cheerick is changed into a Tsaireh מֵ] denotes the proposition *from*, *e. g.*, מִשָּׁמַיִם from heaven, מֵאֶרֶץ from earth. ם suffixed to a noun denotes the possessive pron. 3d pers. pl. masc.

נ prefixed to a verb in the future tense denotes pers. pron. nom. 1st pers. plur.

ן suffixed to the 2d and 3d pers. plur. of a verb in future tense, denotes fut. *optative*. Suffixed to a noun, it denotes possessive pron. 3d pers. pl. fem.

שׁ prefixed to any word, denotes the relative pron. *who, which, that* [Abbreviation of אֲשֶׁר].

ת. The meanings of this letter, as prefix or suffix, are so multifarious that they cannot be reduced to any short rule.†

5. Secondly the alphabet is divided into classes (commonly in five) according to the organs of speech, *i. e.*,

* See note to letter ה.

† מ and ת are frequently prefixed to the infinitive construct of verbs, to change them into nouns, *e. g.* מַתֵּת from תֵּת, תּוֹשָׁב from יָשַׁב.

Gutturals, . . .	א ה ח ע (ר)
Palatals, . . .	ג י כ ק
Linguals, . . .	ד ט ל נ (ר) ת
Dentals (Sibilants) . . .	ז ס צ שׁ שׂ
Labials. . . .	ב ו מ פ
Nasals, ...	מ נ

Letters belonging to the same classes may interchange in a word without altering its meaning, e. g., זָעַק or צָעַק, to cry; צָחַק or שָׂחַק, to laugh; כָּלַט or פָּלַט, to escape.

———◆◆———

§ II.—THE VOWELS.

———

1. Originally, the Hebrew text was written without vowels. Only the three long vowels, ō, ee, and ow, were expressed by the three letters, י ו (ה); א or ה for the long ō, ו for ow, and י for ee. These letters, when serving as vowel bearers, were called vowel letters, but they are frequently omitted. The Massoretes, about the fifth century, invented certain signs, to represent the vowels. They are ten in number; five long and five short ones.

Long.	Short.
1. — Komats,	6. — Pathach,
2. — Tsaireh,	7. — Segol,
3. י — Cheerik,	8. — Cheerik parvum,
4. ו — Chowlom,	9. — Komats chatuf,
5. ו — Shuruk,	10. — Kubbuts.*

N. B.—The names of the five long vowels contain all the ten vowels: the vowel in the first syllable being the long, the one in the second its corresponding short vowel.

2. The three long vowels י—, ו, and ו, may be written with or without the accompanying letter, and yet retain

* 1, like o in home; 2, like a in able; 3, i in machine; 4 ow in vow; 5, u in rule; 6, a in sharp; 7, e in met; 8, i in pin; 9, o in off; 10, u in full.

their long sound, in which case they are called *long and defective;* while in the other case they are called *long and full.*

N. B.—When וֹ is written defective, it is changed into —ִ kubbuts.

3. Hebrew is written and read from right to left, like all Shemitic languages (except Ethiopic); and the consonants are pronounced before the vowels, except the Pathach under ה at the end of a word, e. g., רוּחַ rûach, where the vowel is pronounced before the consonant. It is called *Pathach furtive,* because its position and pronunciation are, as it were, illegitimate.

SH'VA.

4. Any letter which has no vowel is marked by a Sh'va שְׁוָא, which is equal to an apostrophe. This mark is, however, omitted at the end of a word, except in the following three cases.

a. When two vowelless letters come to stand at the end of the word, e. g. יַרְדְּ *yard,* both are marked with Sh'va.

b. The final ךְ has always a Sh'va בָּךְ *boch.*

c. The pers. pron. nom. 2 pers. fem. אַתְּ *at.*

5. As there is a difference between the pronunciation of a vowelless letter at the beginning of a syllable and a vowelless letter at the end of a syllable; the letter in the first case being vocal, and in the latter case quiescent; the grammarians called the Sh'va which marks a vowelless letter at the beginning of a syllable שְׁוָא נָע Sh'va mobile, *i. e.,* Sh'va vocal; and and the Sh'va which marks a vowelless letter at the end of a syllable שְׁוָא נָח Sh'va quiescent, *i. e.* rest.

6. When one of the gutturals, ע, ח, ה, א is to be pronounced at the beginning or middle of a word without a vowel, it gets half a vowel [composite Sh'va], *viz.* —ֲ, —ֱ, or —ֳ *e. g.* אֲשֶׁר ªsher, אֱמֶת ᵉmeth, מָאֳכָל maªchol.

§ III.—DAGHESH.

1. Daghesh, *i. e.*, a point within the letter, is of twofold use:
a. To harden the pronunciations of some letters.
b. To double the letter.
In the first case it is called Daghesh lene, and can occur only in a letter beginning a syllable, and only in the following six letters: ת, פ, כ, ד, ג, ב, (בְּגַד כְּפַת).

2. ב without a daghesh like v; with it בּ like b.
   כ   "   "   "   "   ch;   "   "   כּ   "   k.
   פ   "   "   "   "   ph;   "   "   פּ   "   p.
   ת   "   "   "   "   th;   "   "   תּ   "   t.
The difference in the pronunciation of ג and ד with or without the daghesh is lost.

3. A daghesh in any letter, except the gutturals א, ה, ח, ע and ר, in the middle or at the end of a word, doubles the letter, and is called the daghesh forte.

---•—•—•---

§ IV.—ACCENTS.

1. Every word of the Hebrew text in the Old Testament has an accent. These accents have a threefold use.
a. To mark the tone syllable [which in some words gives a different meaning, *e. g.*, בָּאָה she came, בָּאָה she is coming, something like *désert* and des*ért*.]
b. As interpunctuation, in which case it is the most perfect of all known divisions of sentence; and
c. For cantillation of the Bible in public worship.

2. The use of the accents for the first and second purposes causes them to be divided into two parts, viz., disjunctive and conjunctive accents. Those accents which mark the end of a sentence are called disjunctives; and the rest, conjunctives.

3. The forms and names of the accents are: 1 ⌃ Zarko, 2 ∴ Segol, 3 — Munach, 4 ˙ R'veei, 5 — Mahapach, 6 ˈ Pashto, 7 ⋮ Zokef koten, 8 ⁞ Zokef godel, 9 — Mer-

cho, 10 — Tipcho, 11 — Ethnachto, 12 — Pozer, 13 — T'lisho k'tanoh, 14 — T'lisho g'dowloh, 15 — Kadmoh, 16— V'azlo,
17 — Azlo garash,* 18 — Gershajim, 19 — Dargo, 20 — T'vir,
21 — Y'thiv, 22 | — P'ssick, 23 — Siluk,* 23 — Shalsheleth,
25 — Merchoh k'fuloh, 26 — Karne poroh, 27 — Yerach ben
yowmow.

Of these 27 accents only No. 3, 5, 9, 13, 15, 19, 25, and 27,
are conjunctives; all the rest are disjunctives. The principal
disjunctives, a knowledge of which is absolutely necessary for
proper reading, are the following: — Reveei, — Tipcho,
— Segol, — Zokef katon, — Ethnach, — Siluk, or Soph
possuk.

4. When two or three words have but one accent, the words
without the accent are joined to the accentuated word by a
horizontal line called Makkaf מַקֵּף (־).

5. The accent is generally placed on the ultimate, or penultimate syllable; and when a syllable before the accentuated
one is to be intoned, it gets a perpendicular line under it, called
Metheg מֶתֶג, (i. e. a bridle) (—) e. g., אָנֹכִי. Even the third
vowel before the Metheg takes also a Metheg, e. g.,
מֵאוֹתִיתֵהֶם.

§ V.—ARTICLE.

1. The Hebrew article fully written is הַל, like the Arabic
al; the ל is, however, always dropped, and the first letter of the noun gets a Daghesh compensative. (For the change
of its vowel, see § I., 4, letter ה).

---

*To distinguish between — Pashto and — Kadmo, one must be guided by
the following accent. So by — V'azlo and — Azlo garesh, by the preceding one.

2. It stands only : *a.* as a definite article, never for the inde-
finite ; *b.* as a demonstrative pronoun, thus, *e. g.*, הַלַּיְלָה this
night (Gen. xix. 34.) הַפַּעַם this time (Ex. ix. 27) ; *c.* as a
relative pronoun הַהֹלְכוּא אִתּוֹ who went with him (Josh.
x. 24).

3. When one of the letters לְ, כְ, בְ, is prefixed to a noun with
an article, the whole article disappears, and the prefixed letter
takes the vowel of the article. Thus, instead of בְּהַכֶּסֶף it is
בַּכֶּסֶף in the silver. בָּהָר for בְּהָהָר in the mountain. לָאָדָם
לְהָאָדָם to the man.

4. When the noun has the article, all the following adjectives
and pronouns also have the article. If the noun has the article,
and the adjective has not, then the adjective is a predicate.

§ VI.—NOUN.

1. The Hebrew noun has two genders, and three numbers.
The genders are masculine and feminine ; the numbers, singular, plural, and dual. Masculine are :

a. All living beings of male gender, *e. g.* אַבְרָהָם Abraham,
אַרְיֵה a lion, אָב a father.

b. All names of nations, *e. g.*, עֲמָלֵק Amalek, גּוֹי a nation,
אַשּׁוּר Ashur.

c. All names of seas and rivers, *e. g.*, יָם the sea, נָהָר a river,
יַרְדֵּן the Jordan, פְּרָת Euphrates.

d. Names of mountains, *e. g.*, סִנַי Sinai, תָּבוֹר Tabor.

e. Names of months, *e. g.*, חֹדֶשׁ a month, אָבִיב April, יֶרַח
a month.

f. The names of metals, *e. g.*, זָהָב gold, כֶּסֶף silver, בַּרְזֶל
iron.

N. B.—There is a third gender, which may be called either
e. g., בָּקָר cattle, צֹאן sheep.

2. Feminine nouns are :

a. All living beings of the female gender, *e. g.*, רָחֵל Rachel,
אֵם a mother, פָּרָה a cow.

b. All nouns which end in ◌ָה— *e. g.*, בְּרָכָה a blessing; in ◌ַת—
e. g., דַּעַת knowledge; in ◌ִת— *e. g.*, אַחֲרִית the end; in
◌ֶת— *e. g.*, עֲטֶרֶת a crown; and in ◌וּת— *e. g.*, מַלְכוּת a
kingdom.

c. Names of countries and towns, *e. g.*, עִיר a city, כְּנַעַן
Canaan.

d. All the members of the body, *e. g.*, יָד a hand, רֶגֶל a
foot, אֹזֶן an ear, עַיִן an eye.

3. Nouns of masculine gender form their plural by suffixing
the syllable ◌ִים— *e. g.* דָּבָר a word, דְּבָרִים words, סוּס a horse,
סוּסִים horses. Feminine nouns form their plural by suffixing
◌וֹת, *e. g.* פָּרָה a cow, פָּרוֹת cows, בְּרָכָה a blessing, בְּרָכוֹת
blessings, דַּעַת-דֵּעוֹת.

N.B. The learner will observe that nouns ending in ◌ָה—
lose this termination, and take in its place the plural form ◌וֹת.

4. All nouns which exist by nature or art in pairs, take instead
of the plural a dual form, which ends in ◌ַיִם— *e. g.*, יָד a hand,
יָדַיִם two hands, מֶלְקָחַיִם scales, רֶגֶל a foot, רַגְלַיִם feet.

N. B. When any of the dual nouns assumes either a masculine or a femine plural ending, *e. g.*, יָדוֹת it loses its original
meaning. The word יָדוֹת means *handles;* so רְגָלִים means *times.*

5. There are some masculine nouns which have their plural
in the feminine termination, *e. g.*, אָב a father, אָבוֹת fathers,
מָקוֹם a place, מְקֹמוֹת places; and feminine nouns which
have their plural in the masculine termination, *e. g.* דְּבוֹרָה a
bee, דְּבוֹרִים bees, נְמָלָה an ant, נְמָלִים ants. Some nouns

take their plural in either gender, *e. g.*, דּוֹר a generation, דּוֹרִים or דּוֹרוֹת generations.

N. B.—Masc. nouns which have feminine pl. terminations, and fem. nouns which have masc. pl. terminations, have their adjectives and verbs according to their natural gender, *e. g.*, הָאָבוֹת טוֹבִים the fathers are good, הַדְּבוֹרִים טוֹבוֹת the bees are good.

6. There are some nouns which exist only in plural form and have no singular, *e. g.*, פָּנִים face, זְקֵנִים old age, נְעוּרִים youth, עֲלוּמִים boyhood. Some nouns have only the singular number, and no plural, *e. g.*, שֶׁמֶשׁ sun, זָהָב gold, קַיִץ summer, אָבָק dust. The last mentioned are mainly collective nouns.

7. Proper nouns, *e. g.*, דָּוִד David, אָדָם Adam, have neither the mark of gender nor number. But when a proper noun stands as family name, or national name, *e. g.*, לֵוִי Levy, מִצְרַיִם Mizraim, Egypt, צִידוֹן Zidon, it takes number and gender, *e. g.*, לְוִיִּם Levites, מִצְרִיּוֹת Egyptian women, צִידוֹן צִידוֹנִים, Zidonians.

§ VII.—CONSTRUCT STATE.

1. When two nouns come together and one belongs to, or is defined by the other, [*i. e.* Genit.] the noun possessing or defining remains unchanged, but the noun possessed or defined undergoes the following changes.

2. *a.* Nouns masc. sing. shorten their syllables when constructed to another noun, *e. g.*, דָּבָר a word, דְּבַר מֹשֶׁה word of Moses, זָקֵן an elder, זְקַן בַּיִת elder of the house, לֵבָב a heart, לְבַב אָדָם the heart of man.

b. Nouns in plural masc. drop the last ם and change the preceding Cheerick (—) into Tsaireh (—) *e. g.*, דְּבָרִים words,

דִּבְרֵי מֹשֶׁה words of Moses. זְקֵנִים elders, זִקְנֵי בֵית the elders of the house.

c. Dual construct drops the last ם and (—) and changes the penultimate (—) into (—) *e. g.,* עֵינַיִם two eyes, עֵינֵי אִישׁ eyes of man; שְׂפָתַיִם lips, שִׂפְתֵי חָכָם lips of the wise man.

d. Feminine sing. nouns ending in ה﹘ change the ה into ת and the (—) into (—) *e. g.,* חָכְמָה wisdom, חָכְמַת שְׁלֹמֹה wisdom of Solomon, תּוֹרַת מֹשֶׁה the law of Moses.

e. Feminine plural nouns shorten their second vowel, *e. g.,* abs. בְּרָכוֹת, const. בִּרְכוֹת; abs. עֲלָמוֹת, const. עַלְמוֹת.

N. B.—The noun which is defined stands always before the defining noun and takes no article.

§ VIII.—ADJECTIVE.

1. The adjective stands in Hebrew always after the noun, and must agree with the noun in gender and number, as אִישׁ טוֹב a good man; אִשָּׁה טוֹבָה a good woman; בָּנִים טוֹבִים good sons; בָּנוֹת טוֹבוֹת good daughters.

2. An adjective belonging to two or more nouns (also verbs or participles) must be rendered in the plural number; and if one of the nouns be masculine, the adjective, verb, or participle must be in the masculine gender, *e. g.,* וְאַבְרָהָם וְשָׂרָה זְקֵנִים and Abraham and Sarah were old (Gen. xviii. 11).

3. But when the verb stands before the noun, it is not modified by the nouns which follow, *e. g.,* וַיִּתְחַבֵּא הָאָדָם וְאִשְׁתּוֹ and Adam and his wife hid themselves (Gen. iii. 8), וְלֹא נִמְצָא נָשִׁים יָפוֹת and were not found fine women (Job xlii. 15).

4. When the adjective stands before the noun, or when the noun has an article and the adjective none, the adjective is to be understood as a predicate, *e. g.,* טוֹבָה הָאָרֶץ the land is good, אֶרֶץ טוֹבָה a good land, הָאָרֶץ טוֹבָה the land i⸱

good, הָאָרֶץ הַטּוֹבָה the good land, אֶרֶץ הַטּוֹבָה the *good* land. In the last case the emphasis lies on the adjective.

5. Comparative and superlative of the Hebrew adjectives, verbs, particles, and pronouns are formed in the following manner:

When two nouns are compared in the positive form, the letter כ is prefixed to both nouns, e. g., וְהָיָה כָעָם כַּכֹּהֵן כַּעֶבֶד כַּאדֹנָיו כַּשִּׁפְחָה כַּגְבִרְתָּהּ. And it shall be as with the people, so with the priest; as with the servant, so with the master; as with the maid, so with the mistress (Is. xxiv. 2). In the comparative, the letter מ with a (—) before the noun with which it is compared, e. g., טוֹב שֵׁם מִשֶּׁמֶן טוֹב וְיוֹם הַמָּוֶת מִיּוֹם הִוָּלְדוֹ. A good name is better than precious ointment, and the day of death than the day of one's birth (Eccl. vii. 1), עָרוּם מִכֹּל more subtile than all (Gen. iii. 1) הַטּוֹבָה מִמֶּנָּה, better than she (Esther i. 19).

The superlative is formed, *a.* by repeating the adjective, e. g., קֹדֶשׁ קָדָשִׁים most holy; *b.* by adding the word מְאֹד, e. g., טוֹב מְאֹד very good; *c.* by putting the article before the adjective, and the letter ב before the noun with which it is compared, e. g., הַיָּפָה בַּנָּשִׁים the most beautiful among the women, הַדַּל בִּמְנַשֶּׁה the poorest in (the tribe of) Menasse.

N. B.—When the superlative is expressed by a verb, the word כֹל with the prefix מ is put before the noun with which it is compared, e. g., וַיֶּחְכַּם שְׁלֹמֹה מִכָּל־אָדָם And Solomo was wiser than all men.

IX.—PRONOUNS.

1. The Hebrew pronouns are of two kinds:
a. Separable, consisting of distinct words.
b. Inseparable words, i. e., letters suffixed to nouns and verbs. Separable pronouns are, 1. personal; 2. relative; 3. demon-

LIBRAR
UNIVERSITY
CALIFORNI

strative ; and 4. interrogative. The inseparable pronouns are,
5. possessive ; 6. passive ; both expressed by the letters ה,ו,י,
נ. ם, כ (הַכִּנוּיִם pronouns) suffixed to nouns and verbs.

2. PERSONAL PRONOUNS.

Inst.	Abl.	Ac.	D.	G.	N.	
בִּי	מִמֶּנִּי	אוֹתִי	לִי	שֶׁלִּי	אֲנִי or אָנֹכִי	1. c. sin.
בְּךָ	מִמְּךָ	אוֹתְךָ	לְךָ	שֶׁלְּךָ	אַתָּה	2. m.
בָּךְ	מִמֵּךְ	אוֹתָךְ	לָךְ	שֶׁלָּךְ	אַתְּ	2. fem.
בּוֹ	מִמֶּנּוּ	אוֹתוֹ	לוֹ	שֶׁלּוֹ	הוּא	3. m.
בָּהּ	מִמֶּנָּה	אוֹתָהּ	לָהּ	שֶׁלָּהּ	הִיא	3. fem.
בָּנוּ	מִמֶּנּוּ	אוֹתָנוּ	לָנוּ	שֶׁלָּנוּ	אֲנַחְנוּ	1. c. pl.
בָּכֶם	מִכֶּם	אֶתְכֶם	לָכֶם	שֶׁלָּכֶם	אַתֶּם	2. m.
בָּכֶן	מִכֶּן	אֶתְכֶן	לָכֶן	שֶׁלָּכֶן	אַתֶּן	2. fem.
בָּהֶם	מֵהֶם	אֶתְהֶם	לָהֶם	שֶׁלָּהֶם	הֵם	3. m.
בָּהֶן	מֵהֶן	אֶתְהֶן	לָהֶן	שֶׁלָּהֶן	הֵן	3. fem.

3. The relative pronoun for all genders and numbers is אֲשֶׁר
or שֶׁ, who, that, which.

4. The demonstrative pronoun is:

זֶה this, masculine.   אֵל)
זֹאת this, feminine.   אֵלֶּה } these, plural com.

זוּ, הַלָּז, that or this, common.

5. The interrogative pronoun is מִי who? (personal), מַה,
מֶה, מֶה which? (things).

N. B.—The demonstrative pronoun is also used without
having its proper signification, e. g., לָמָּה זֶה אָנֹכִי why am
I thus? (Gen. xxv. 22.) קוֹל דּוֹדִי הִנֵּה זֶה בָּא The voice
of my beloved! behold, he cometh (Cant. ii. 8).

6. The possessive pronoun is a syllable of one or more letters

19

suffixed to a noun in singular or plural, to denote whose object it is, *e. g.,* סֵפֶר a book, סִפְרִי my book.

7. The possessive pronominal suffixes are:

To a Singular Noun:

a plural pronoun.					a singular pronoun.				
3. person fem.	3. person masc.	2. person feu.	2 person mase.	1. pers. com.	3. pers. 3. fem.	pers. m.	2. pers. fem.	2. pers. m.	1. pers. com.
־ֶן	־ָם	־ְכֶן	־ְכֶם	־ֵנוּ	־ָהּ	־וֹ	־ֵךְ	־ְךָ	־ִי

To a Plural Noun.

־ֵיהֶן	־ֵיהֶם	־ֵיכֶן	־ֵיכֶם	־ֵינוּ	־ֶיהָ	־ָיו	־ַיִךְ	־ֶיךָ	־ַי
their	their	your	your	our	hers	his	thine	thine	my

Example to a Masculine Noun.

abs. דָּבָר a word; construct state דְּבַר.

דְּבָרָהּ	דְּבָרוֹ	דְּבָרֶךָ	דְּבָרְךָ	דְּבָרִי
her word	l is word	thy word	thy word	my word
דְּבָרָן	דְּבָרָם	דְּבַרְכֶן	דְּבַרְכֶם	דְּבָרֵנוּ
their word	their word	your word	your word	our word

abs. דְּבָרִים words; construct state דִּבְרֵי.

דִּבְרֶיהָ	דְּבָרָיו	דְּבָרֶיךָ	דְּבָרַיִךְ	דְּבָרַי
her words	his words	thy words	thy words	my words
דִּבְרֵיהֶן	דִּבְרֵיהֶם	דִּבְרֵיכֶן	דִּבְרֵיכֶם	דְּבָרֵינוּ
their words	their words	your words	your words	our words

Example to a Feminine Noun.

תּוֹרָה a law; construct state תּוֹרַת.

תּוֹרָתָהּ	תּוֹרָתוֹ	תּוֹרָתֶךָ	תּוֹרָתְךָ	תּוֹרָתִי
her law	his law	thy law	thy law	my law
תּוֹרָתָן	תּוֹרָתָם	תּוֹרַתְכֶן	תּוֹרַתְכֶם	תּוֹרָתֵנוּ
their law	their law	your law	your law	our law

תּוֹרוֹת laws; construct state the same.

תּוֹרוֹתֶיהָ	תּוֹרוֹתָיו	תּוֹרוֹתֶיךָ	תּוֹרוֹתַיִךְ	תּוֹרוֹתַי
her laws	his laws	thy laws	thy laws	my laws
תּוֹרוֹתֵיהֶן	תּוֹרוֹתֵיהֶם	תּוֹרוֹתֵיכֶן	תּוֹרוֹתֵיכֶם	תּוֹרוֹתֵינוּ
their laws	their laws	your laws	your laws	our laws

8. The passive pronouns are the same suffixes as those of the nouns, appended to the verb; in which they are objective, instead of possessive pronouns. A table of them will be found among the verbs.

§ X.—NUMERATION.

1. Numeration is divided in units, tens, hundreds, thousands, etc.; and the letters of the alphabet are used to represent them. (See the alphabet table.) To express 1,000 by letters א with a dot over it א is used, בּ 2,000, גּ 3,000, דּ 4,000, הּ 5,000, etc. Thus we now figure the present year of the creation, shortly, ה ת׳ר׳ל׳ז 5637*.

2. Numbers are divided into cardinals and ordinals. The cardinals have masc. and fem. absolute and construct. The ordinal numbers have two genders, but no construct state. The numbers have also pronominal suffixes, e. g., שְׁנֵינוּ us two (Gen. xxxi. 37), שְׁלָשְׁתְּכֶם you three (Numb. xii. 47).

CARDINAL NUMBERS.

Feminine.		Masculine.		
Construct.	Absolute.	Construct.	Absolute.	
אַחַת	אַחַת	אַחַד	אֶחָד	1.
שְׁתֵּי	שְׁתַּיִם	שְׁנֵי	שְׁנַיִם	2.
שְׁלֹשׁ, שְׁלָשׁ	שָׁלֹשׁ	שְׁלֹשֶׁת	שְׁלֹשָׁה	3.
אַרְבַּע	אַרְבַּע	אַרְבַּעַת	אַרְבָּעָה	4.
חֲמֵשׁ	חָמֵשׁ	חֲמֵשֶׁת	חֲמִשָּׁה	5.
שֵׁשׁ	שֵׁשׁ	שֵׁשֶׁת	שִׁשָּׁה	6.
שְׁבַע	שֶׁבַע	שִׁבְעַת	שִׁבְעָה	7.
שְׁמוֹנֶה	שְׁמוֹנֶה	שְׁמוֹנַת	שְׁמוֹנָה	8.
תְּשַׁע	תֵּשַׁע	תְּשַׁעַת	תִּשְׁעָה	9.
עֶשֶׂר	עֶשֶׂר	עֲשֶׂרֶת	עֲשָׂרָה	10.

* To find the year of the Jewish calendar, you have but to subtract 240 from the Christian era, thus: 1877—240—1637, and add 4000—5637.

4. From ten to twenty, the number ten has its proper gender termination, viz.: masc. without הָ— and fem. with הָ—. Some of the units stand in the absolute and some in construct state.

FEMININE.	MASCULINE.
11. { אַחַת עֶשְׂרֵה / עַשְׁתֵּי	{ אַחַד עָשָׂר / עַשְׁתֵּי עָשָׂר
12. { שְׁתֵּים עֶשְׂרֵה / שְׁתֵּי	{ שְׁנִים עָשָׂר / שְׁנֵי
13. שְׁלֹשׁ עֶשְׂרֵה	שְׁלֹשָׁה עָשָׂר
14. אַרְבַּע עֶשְׂרֵה	אַרְבָּעָה עָשָׂר
15. חֲמֵשׁ עֶשְׂרֵה	חֲמִשָּׁה עָשָׂר
16. שֵׁשׁ עֶשְׂרֵה	שִׁשָּׁה עָשָׂר
17. שְׁבַע עֶשְׂרֵה	שִׁבְעָה עָשָׂר
18. שְׁמוֹנֶה עֶשְׂרֵה	שְׁמוֹנָה עָשָׂר
19. תְּשַׁע עֶשְׂרֵה	תִּשְׁעָה עָשָׂר

N. B.—It will be observed that number 11, m. as well as fem., is used only in the construct state; 12, in construct as well as in absolute state. From 13 to 19, inclusive, the masc. in absolute, the fem. in constr.

5. The numbers 20 to 90 are formed by יִם— suffixed to עֶשְׂר in the number 20, and the same suffix יִם— to the constr. masc. unit numbers, e. g., שְׁלֹשִׁים 30, אַרְבָּעִים 40. If a unit is added, the unit is used in the absolute with the ו conjunctive, e. g., אַרְבָּעָה וַחֲמִשִּׁים 54, אֶחָד וְעֶשְׂרִים 21, etc.

6. The hundreds have always the feminine termination: מֵאָה 100, plural מֵאוֹת; the units which number the hundreds are the same as are used in the fem. cardinal numbers from 13 to 19, e. g., שְׁלֹשׁ מֵאוֹת 300. The thousands have the masc. termination, e. g., שֵׁשֶׁת אֲלָפִים 6,000, אַרְבַּעַת אֲלָפִים 4,000.

N. B.—Two hundred, two thousand, and two ten thousands

take the dual form, *e. g.*, רְבוֹאתַיִם 2,000, אֲלָפִים 200, מָאתַיִם 20,000. רְבָבָה, plural רְבָבוֹת, means, a great multitude; ־רְבוֹאת 10,000, plural רִבּוֹא

7. The ordinal numbers are in all cases like the adjective, and have both numbers and genders ; they must agree with the noun.

FEMININE.		MASCULINE.		
Plural.	Singular.	Plural.	Singular.	No.
רִאשׁוֹנוֹת	רִאשׁוֹנָה	רִאשׁוֹנִים	רִאשׁוֹן	1st.
שְׁנִיּוֹת	שֵׁנִית	שְׁנִיִּים	שֵׁנִי	2d.
שְׁלִישִׁיּוֹת	שְׁלִישִׁית	שְׁלִישִׁים	שְׁלִישִׁי	3d.
רְבִיעִיּוֹת	רְבִיעִית	רְבִיעִים	רְבִיעִי	4th.
חֲמִישִׁיּוֹת	חֲמִישִׁית	חֲמִישִׁים	חֲמִישִׁי	5th.
שִׁשִּׁיּוֹת	שִׁשִּׁית	שִׁשִּׁים	שִׁשִּׁי	6th.
שְׁבִיעִיּוֹת	שְׁבִיעִית	שְׁבִיעִים	שְׁבִיעִי	7th.
שְׁמִינִיּוֹת	שְׁמִינִית	שְׁמִינִים	שְׁמִינִי	8th.
תְּשִׁיעִיּוֹת	תְּשִׁיעִית	תְּשִׁיעִים	תְּשִׁיעִי	9th.
עֲשִׂירִיּוֹת	עֲשִׂירִית	עֲשִׂירִים	עֲשִׂירִי	10th.

N. B.—From 10 upward the cardinal and ordinal numbers are the same.

8. The fractional number are from three to ten, inclusive, the same as the ordinal numbers sing. fem. *Half* is expressed by מַחֲצִית , חֵצִי , חֲצִי·

§ XI.—THE VERB.

1. The Hebrew verb consists of three radical letters ; and where these three letters are written and pronounced as consonants, through all paradigms and tenses, it is called a *regular verb*. But when any one of the three radical letters is either omitted or not pronounced, it is an *irregular verb*. The irregular verbs are of two classes :

a. Imperfect, *i. e.*, when one letter is omitted.

b. When the letters are all written, but not pronounced which are called quiescent verbs. (For particulars see § XI. 2.)

2. The Hebrew verb has 7 voices, or paradigms.

1. פָּעַל (he wrought) or קַל (light), because this voice is unburdened by any additional letter or daghesh, denotes the simple *active*.

2. נִפְעַל (he was wrought upon) characterized by a prefixed נ or by a daghesh in the first radical letter, denotes the simple *passive*.

N. B.—The Nifal form cannot be made of *intransitive* verbs, yet it can stand as a *deponent*, signifying Kal, *e. g.*, נִלְחַם he warred, fought, נִשְׁעַן he leaned. Such verbs have generally no Kal form at all. In some verbs Kal and Nifal have the same meaning, *e. g.*, הָלַךְ, נֶהֱלַךְ he went, קָרַב and נִקְרַב he approached, חָלָה, נֶחְלָה he was sick. In some verbs Nifal has the meaning of the Hithpael, *i. e.*, reflective, *e. g.*, יִפָּרֵד he will divide himself, etc.

3. פִּעֵל (he wrought diligently) characterized by a daghesh in the second radical, denotes the intensive active.

N. B.—When Piel is made of a verb which is in Kal intransitive, it denotes in Piel the transitive, *i. e.*, שָׂמֵחַ to be glad, שִׂמַּח he made glad. In some verbs the Piel has the opposite meaning of Kal, *e. g.*, סָקַל he stoned, סִקֵּל he removed the stones.

4. פֻּעַל (he was diligently wrought upon) characterized by a shooruck —, under the first radical, and a daghesh in the second radical, denotes the intensive passive.

N. B.—Some verbs have their active in Kal, and their passive in Pual, *e. g.*, רָחַץ he washed, רֻחַץ he was washed. In the same way we find verbs which have their active in Piel, and

their passive in Nifal, *e. g.*, נִחַם he comforted, הִנָּחֵם to be comforted. (Psalm lxxiii. 3.)

5. הִפְעִיל (he caused another to work), characterized by הַ prefixed and a י between the second and third radicals, denotes causative active.

N. B.—There are some verbs used only in Hifil form, *e. g.*, הַשְׁכֵּם to rise early, הִבִּיט he looked, הִכָּה he smote, הִשְׁלִיךְ he cast down.

6. הָפְעַל (he was caused to work). It is characterized by הָ prefixed, and denotes the causative passive.

7. הִתְפַּעֵל (he wrought on himself), characterized by הִת prefixed and a daghesh in the second radical, denotes the reflexive. Some verbs have in Hithpael the same meaning as in Kal, *e. g.*, הִתְהַלֵּךְ and הָלַךְ he went, הִתְקוֹמֵם, קוּם, to arise against one.

2. When the first radical is one of the letters, שׂ, שׁ, ס, the characteristic ת of Hithpael changes its place with the first radical, as הִסְתַּכֵּל "he feigned himself drunk," for הִתְסַכֵּל; הִשְׁתַּמֵּר "he guarded himself," for הִתְשַׁמֵּר, for euphony's sake.

3. When the first radical is ד, ט, or ת, the characteristic ת is omitted, and compensated by a daghesh in the first radical, *e. g.*, הִתָּהֵר, הִטָּהֵר for אִדַּמֶּה, אֶתְדַּמֶּה for.

4. The Hebrew verb is varied by moods, tenses, numbers, persons, and genders. There are three moods: 1. The *indicative*, describing the action as done with certainty, *e. g.*, לָמַדְתָּ thou hast learned. There is, however, also a conjunctive, which is chiefly formed by the words, לוּלֵי, לוּ, and פֶּן : לוּ יִשְׁמָעֵאל יִחְיֶה לְפָנֶיךָ "Oh, that Ishmael might live before thee!" (Gen. xvii. 18), פֶּן יִטְרֹף Lest he tear (Ps. vii. 3). 2. The *imperative*, commanding a thing to be done. This mood can

also be made a *precative*, either by suffixing ה *e. g.*, שׁוּבָה
Oh, turn! or by adding the particle נָא, *e. g.*, זְכֹר נָא Oh,
remember! Sometimes by using both forms together, *e. g.*,
הוֹשִׁיעָה נָא Oh, save (Psalm xviii. 25). 3. The *infinitive* mood,
simply speaking of an action without any regard to time. It
is used sometimes only to give force to an action.

5. The *tenses* in the Hebrew verb are three: The past, or
preterit, expressing a thing already done; imperfect and pluperfect are included, and are to be understood by the context
of the sentence. 2. The progressive present, of which there
are two, the present participle and the past participle. (See
table I.) 3. The future, declaring the action yet to be done.
The past in the future is expressed by the simple past, *e. g.*,
וּמוֹלַדְתְּךָ אֲשֶׁר הוֹלַדְתָּ אַחֲרֵיהֶם but thy chidren which thou
shalt have born after them. (Gen. xlv. 6.)

6. The Hebrew verb has three persons:
a. The person speaking.
b. The person spoken to.
c. The person spoken of.

Two genders, masculine and feminine, and two numbers,
singular and plural. When anything impersonal is related,
the 3d person sing. masc. is used, *e. g.*, וַיֹּאמֶר לְיוֹסֵף and one
told Joseph. (Gen. xlviii. 1.)

§ XII.—IRREGULAR VERBS.

1. The first class of the irregular verbs is the *imperfect*.
(See § X. 1). Those verbs of which the first radical is נ and
י are imperfect, חֲסֵרִים, *i. e.*, the נ and י will be omitted, and
the second radical takes then a daghesh, *e. g.*, נָתַן he gave,
יִתֵּן he will give; יָצַק he poured, יִצַּק he will pour.

2. The second class of irregular verbs is called *quiescents*,
נֵחִים, *i. e.*, the letters are written, but are not pronounced.*

---

* The Hebrew Grammarians made use of the three letters פ ע ל to designate
the three radical letters of any verb. The 1st they call פ, the 2d ע, the 3d ל.
So instead of saying: the first radical is א, they say: it is a verb פ״א, etc.

These verbs are:

1. פ"א, when the first radical is א, e. g. אָבַל
2. פ"י, " " " " " י, " " יֵשֵׁב
3. ע"ו, " " second " " ו, " " קוּם
4. ע"י, " " " " " י, " " בִּין
5. ל"א, " " third " " א, " " מָצָא
6. ל"ה, " " " " " ה, " " גָּלָה
7. ע"ע, when the 2d and 3d letters are the same סָבַב

3. There is a third class of irregular verbs, called *guttural*, i. e., when one of the radicals is ר, ע, ח, in which case there is caused a deviation from the usual vowel pointing of the verb.

4. Some verbs are quadriliteral, as כִּרְבֵּל to gird, כִּרְסֵם to cut off, פִּרְשֵׂז to expand. Also the piel of some verbs ע"ו and ע"ע appear in quadriliteral form, as טִלְטֵל to prostrate, from טוּל, to throw, שִׁעֲשַׁע to delight, from שָׁעָה, or שָׁעַע.

§ XIII.—PASSIVE PRONOUNS OF VERBS.

1. The active verb takes a double pronominal suffix, first to denote the number and person, second the objective or accusative case, as they suffer the action of the verb to which they are joined; thus שְׁמַרְתִּיהָ I have kept her, תִּי I, הָ her; תִּי being the agent, הָ the patient. (See Table.)

2. The *infinitive* takes the pronominal suffix of the possessive, as well as the objective, e. g., בְּקָרְאִי in my calling, בְּבָרְחוֹ in his fleeing, בְּהִבָּרְאָם in creating them, לְעָבְדָהּ to work her. The *participle* takes the objective suffix in the like manner.

3. The pronominal objective suffixes are sometimes to be rendered as if they were detached pronouns governed by a preposition understood, thus, נְתַתָּנִי thou gavest *unto* me.

(Josh. xv. 16.) חָנֵּנוּ be favorable *unto* us, יְגָרְךָ shall dwell *with* thee (Psalm v. 5).

---

§ XIV.—ADVERBS OR PARTICLES.

1. אַחַר	after,	takes	the	suffix	of	noun	plural.
אַיֵּה, אֵי	where ?	"	"	"	"	"	"
אֵין	not,	"	"	"	"	"	sing.
אֶל	to, against,	"	"	"	"	"	plural.
אֶפֶס	none, but	"	"	"	"	"	sing.
אֵצֶל	near, beside,	"	"	"	"	"	"
אֵת	with,	"	"	"	"	"	"
בִּגְלַל	because,	"	"	"	"	"	"
בֵּין	between,	"	"	"	"	"	"
בִּלְעַד	besides,	"	"	"	"	"	plural.
בִּלְתִּי	except,	"	"	"	"	"	sing.
בַּעֲבוּר	for the sake of	"	"	"	"	"	"
הֵן	lo, behold,	"	"	"	"	"	"
זוּלַת	only,	"	"	"	"	"	"
כְּמוֹ	as, like,	"	"	"	"	"	"
לְבַד	apart,	"	"	"	"	"	"
לְמַעַן	because of,	"	"	"	"	"	"
לְעֻמַּת	opposite,	"	"	"	"	"	"
לִפְנֵי	before,	"	"	"	"	"	plural.
מִן	from, out of,	"	"	"	"	"	sing.
מוּל	opposite,	"	"	"	"	"	"
נֶגֶד	before, opposite,	"	"	"	"	"	"
נוֹכַח	" "	"	"	"	"	"	"
סָבִיב	round about,	"	"	"	"	"	plural.

עַד unto, takes the suffix of noun plural.

עוֹד yet, " " " " " sing.

עַל upon, " " " " " plural.

עִם with, " " " " " sing.

תַּחַת under, instead, " " " " " "

2. Adverbs or particles which take no suffix: אוֹ or, either; אָז, אֲזַי then, at that time; אֵיכָה, אֵיךְ, אֵיכָה how; אַךְ only, surely; אָכֵן id.; אָנָה, אֵיפֹה, אֵי, אַיֵּה where; אוּלַי perhaps, peradventure; אִם if; אוּלָם but; אָן whither; אַיִן nothing; אַף also; כַּאֲשֶׁר as, according; אֲבָל yet; אָמְנָם verily; אַט slowly; אַל not; אִלּוּ if; אָמֵן so be it; בַּל not; בְּלִי without; כֹּה here; בָּכָה in that manner; גַּם also; הֵיךְ how; הָלְאָה beyond; הֵנָּה, הֲלֹם hither; חוּץ except; טֶרֶם not yet; יַחְדָּיו together; יַעַן because; כְּבָר long ago; כָּכָה, כֹּה so; כִּי or, if, perhaps, because; כֵּן so, thus; כַּמָּה how much; how many; לֹא not; מִבְּלִי without; מַדּוּעַ wherefore; מַהֵר quickly; מְאוּמָה something, anything; מָחָר to-morrow; מַטָּה below; מְעַט a little; מַעַל above; מָתַי when; נָא now; נֶצַח eternal; עַד unto; עֲדִי id.; עֻמַּת over against; עַתָּה now; עֵקֶב because; פֹּה here; פֶּן lest, that not; פִּתְאֹם suddenly; קֶדֶם in past time; קָרוֹב closely; רַב much, many; רֶגַע momentary; רֵיקָם emptily; רַק only, but; שָׁוְא vainly; שִׁלְשׁוֹם the day before yesterday; שָׁם there; בְּשַׁגַּם because of; תְּמוֹל yesterday; תָּמִיד always, continually.

§ XV.—INTERJECTIONS.

Sounds of one or more syllables, used when experiencing joy or pain, are called interjections. They being natural expressions, are almost in all languages the same. When the

expression is of joy, the sounds הֵדָד ! הֶאָח ! are used ; of pain or lamentation the words הָהּ ! אֲהָהּ ! אוֹיָה ! אוֹי ! אַלְלַי ! אֲבוֹי ! הוֹי ! are used. For request or petition the words נָא ! בִּי ! are used.

---

§ XVI.—SYNTAX.—NOUNS.

1. When several nouns come to stand in a sentence, they are all either alike *i. e.*, subjects or objects, or they are not of the same case. They may be all subjects having the same predicate, *e. g.*, יַעֲקֹב וְכָל־זַרְעוֹ אִתּוֹ : בָּנָיו וּבְנֵי בָנָיו אִתּוֹ בְּנֹתָיו וּבְנוֹת בָּנָיו Jacob and his seed with him: his sons, and his sons' sons with him, his daughters and his sons' daughters (Gen. xlvi. 6, 7). Also as objects, *e. g.*, וַיִּקַּח חֶמְאָה וְחָלָב וּבֶן הַבָּקָר And he took butter and milk and the calf (Gen. xviii. 8). Or all the nouns in the sentence may denote one object, *c. g.*, אֲנָשִׁים חֲכָמִים וּנְבֹנִים וִידֻעִים Wise men and understanding, and known (Deut. i. 13). Lastly one noun may define the other, *e. g.*, בֵּית פַּרְעֹה מֶלֶךְ מִצְרָיִם The house of Paraoh, king of Egypt.

2. When several nouns are in a sentence as subjects, they need not necessarily be of the same gender and number, although they are in the same relation ; the verb and adjective are then generally in plural masculine, yet when the verb stands at the beginning, before the nouns, the verb can be in masc. sing., *e. g.*, וְאַבְרָהָם וְשָׂרָה זְקֵנִים בָּאִים בַּיָּמִים Now Abraham and Sarah were old, well stricken with age (Gen. xviii. 11). וַיָּבֹא אַהֲרֹן וְכָל זִקְנֵי יִשְׂרָאֵל And he came, Aaron and all the elders of Israel (Exod. xviii. 12). Generally the verb is governed by the chief person in the sentence.

3. Sometimes, when the verb stands before the noun, it is regarded as *impersonal*, and agrees with the following noun neither in gender nor in number, *e. g.*, וְלֹא נִמְצָא נָשִׁים יָפוֹת

And it was not found beautiful women (Job xlii. 15), כִּי יִהְיֶה
נַעֲרָה if there be a virgin (Deut. xxii. 23).

4. The conjunction of several nouns in the same sentence
is done either by placing the וֹ copulative before every noun,
as וְעַבְדוֹ וַאֲמָתוֹ וְשׁוֹרוֹ וַחֲמוֹרוֹ and his man-servant, and his
maid-servant, and his ox, and his ass (Ex. xx. 14), or before the
last noun, as רְאוּבֵן שִׁמְעוֹן לֵוִי וִיהוּדָה Reuben, Simeon,
Levy and Jehudah (Ex. i. 2.), or by placing the conjunc. before
the second and fourth nouns: דָּן וְנַפְתָּלִי גָּד וְאָשֵׁר Dan and
Naphthali, Gad and Asher; and when there are three nouns,
only before the last.

5. When several nouns stand in predicate, all must have the
same sign, אֶת־קְרָשָׁיו וְאֶת־קְרָסָיו אֶת־בְּרִיחָיו וְאֶת־עַמּוּדָיו
וְאֶת־אֲדָנָיו His taches, and his boards, his bars, his pillars,
and his sockets (Ex. xxxv. 11). לְךָ וּלְעַבְדְּךָ וְלַאֲמָתֶךָ
וְלִשְׂכִירְךָ וּלְתוֹשָׁבְךָ For thee and for thy servant, and for
thy maid, and for thy hired servant, and for thy stranger that
sojourneth with thee (Levit. xxv. 6). The same is the case
with all the propositions.

6. When one object has several adjectives, they must all
agree with the object. (See § VIII. 1.) But when the object
is constructed to the adjective, it is not modified.

7. Nouns belonging to one subject, which are explanatory
of one another, if they stand before the subject, must have the
same mark as the subject, e. g., אֶת־בִּנְךָ אֶת־יְחִידְךָ אֶת־
יִצְחָק Thy son, thy only one, Isaac (Gen. xxii. 2). אֶל אָחִיךָ
אֶל עֵשָׂו to thy brother, to Esau (ibid. xxxii. 6). But when
the subject precedes, the other nouns need not stand in the
same case, e. g., בְּרָחֵל בְּבִתְּךָ not בְּרָחֵל בִּתְּךָ הַקְּטַנָּה ·

§ XVII.—CONSTRUCT STATE.

1. When any idea is to be expressed in Hebrew by two
words, it is formed by the first noun being constructed to the

second. (See § VII. 1). The second noun is then defining the first, as: קִרְיָה a town, שָׂדֶה a field, קִרְיַת מֶלֶךְ royal city, residence, שְׂדֵה הַמַּכְפֵּלָה the Machpelah field. This construct form can occur in an active as well as in a passive subject. Often we find two synonyms in construct state, as יְרַק עֵשֶׂב green herb, מְלֶאכֶת עֲבוֹדָה work of labor, מְנָת חֶלְקִי part of my portion.

2. The words בָּנִים, בְּעָלָה, בַּעַל, בֵּן, בַּת, אִשָּׁה, אִישׁ, אֲנָשִׁים, בָּנוֹת, are often constructed with an abstract, to form an adjective, as אִישׁ תְּבוּנוֹת a wise man, אֵשֶׁת חַיִל a valiant woman, בֶּן־מָוֶת a condemned man (to death) בַּת שָׁנָה a (woman) year old, בֶּן־קֶשֶׁת an arrow (lit. the son of the bow).

3. A noun can be constructed to another noun, adjective and a demonstrative pronoun, as אֶל מְקוֹם זֶה to this place, עֹשֵׂה אֵלֶּה doer of these. It can also be constructed to a numeral, e. g., בֶּן אַרְבָּעִים son of forty (forty years old). The noun can never be constructed to a particle or verb, except by ellipsis, e. g., מְקוֹם אֲשֶׁר אֲסִירֵי הַמֶּלֶךְ אֲסוּרִים שָׁם where it is to be read as מְקוֹם אֲסִירִים אֲשֶׁר also תְּחִלַּת הַנְּבוּאָה אֲשֶׁר which is to be read תְּחִלַּת דְּבַר ה׳ דבר. Also to a particle, when the particle is regarded as a substantive, as וּדְבַר מַה־יַּרְאֵנִי and whatsoever he sheweth me (Numb. xxiii. 3). Neither can a noun be constructed to a noun with a proposition.

4. When a noun is constructed to several nouns, it is repeated when the nouns are of different kinds, but when they are of the same kind, the construct noun is not repeated, e. g., בִּפְרִי בִטְנְךָ וּבִפְרִי בְהֶמְתְּךָ וּבִפְרִי אַדְמָתֶךָ the noun is every time repeated; אֶרֶץ חִטָּה וּשְׂעֹרָה וְגֶפֶן וּתְאֵנָה וְרִמּוֹן the noun is not repeated.

Often there are several nouns in the construct state, as פְּרִי גְדָל לְכַב מֶלֶךְ אַשּׁוּר in which case one noun explains the other, but two or more separate nouns cannot be constructed to one noun. Thus you cannot say : חָכְמַת וּתְבוּנַת · but must say : חָכְמַת אָדָם וּתְבוּנָתוֹ ·

§ XVIII.—PECULIAR USE OF THE NOUN.

1. The Hebrew uses sometimes the same noun twice, either in the same gender and number, or in different numbers. If it is used in the same number, it has the significance of *every one*, as, אִישׁ אִישׁ מִבֵּית יִשְׂרָאֵל *every* man of the house of Israel, יוֹם יוֹם *every* day, daily. Secondly, *emphasis*, as צֶדֶק צֶדֶק תִּרְדֹּף Righteousness, righteousness follow. מִזְבֵּחַ מִזְבֵּחַ O altar, altar! (1 Kings xiii. 2). When two nouns are united by ו conjunctive it signifies a diversity between the two nouns, as מְדִינָה וּמְדִינָה כִּכְתָבָהּ וְעַם וָעָם כִּלְשׁוֹנוֹ This land and that land as it writes, and one people or another people as it speaks (Esth. i. 22). בְּלֵב וָלֵב יְדַבֵּרוּ with a double heart do they speak. But when the first noun is in singular and the second in plural, it denotes the superlative, as מֶלֶךְ מְלָכִים king of kings, *i. e.*, the highest king, likewise קֹדֶשׁ קָדָשִׁים holy of holiness, *i. e.*, the most holy (See § VIII. 5).

§ XIX.—RELATION OF THE ADJECTIVE. ADVERB AND VERB TO THE NOUNS.

1. The verb, adverb, and adjective must agree with the noun in gender and number (See § VIII. 1). And in construct state the adverb or adjective must agree with the noun constructed, as יִרְאַת יְ"י טְהוֹרָה the fear of the Lord is pure. The adverb טְהוֹרָה is therefore fem. because the construct יִרְאַת is fem.

2. When several nouns of various genders belong to one verb, the verb is used in the gender of the most prominent noun, e. g., וַתִּכְתֹּב אֶסְתֵּר הַמַּלְכָּה וּמָרְדְּכַי הַיְּהוּדִי And *she* wrote Esther the queen and Mordechai the Jew (Esth. ix. 20), Esther being the chief person. הַחָכְמָה וְהַמַּדַּע נָתוּן לָךְ Wisdom and knowledge is granted unto thee (2 Chron. i. 12). The second noun מַדַּע being of a higher degree, the verb agrees with in.

3. Sometimes the noun is in plural and the verb in singular, and this for two reasons. 1) Because there is an ellipsis, as וְיֵשׁ מִשְׁפָּטֶיךָ where it is to be understood, כָּל אַחַת כָּל אַחַת מִכָּנוֹת צָעֲדָה is בָּנוֹת צָעֲדָה also מִמִּשְׁפָּטֶיךָ יָשַׁר 2) Lies it in the imagination of the writer, seeing each of the בָּנוֹת singly mounting the wall (Gen. xlix. 22).

4. Where the noun constructed has the same meaning as the noun to which it is constructed, or where one noun can be left out entirely, the verb agrees with the second noun, as נֶגַע צָרַעַת כִּי תִהְיֶה When the plague of leprosy will be (Lev. xiii. 9). The noun נֶגַע though it is masc., the verb is yet in fem. תִהְיֶה, because the nouns could be inverted, or the first noun left out altogether. So in וְצַפַּחַת הַשֶּׁמֶן לֹא חָסֵר Neither did the cruse of oil fail (1 Kings xvii. 16); the construct צַפַּחַת feminine, yet the verb חָסֵר in masc., because it refers to the *oil*, not to the cruse.

5. The adverb and adjective belonging to a *collective* noun, can be in sing. as well as in plur. It is in sing. when it refers to the whole, as עַם גָּדוֹל וָרָב A people great and many (Deut. iii. 21), but in plur. when it refers to each individual, as וְהָעָם עָלוּ מִן הַיַּרְדֵּן And the people came up out of Jordan (Josh. iv. 19), where every individual is meant.

6. Some nouns have only the pl. number, as פָּנִים face,

חַיִּים lite, מַיִם water, שָׁמַיִם * and the verb, adverb, or
adjective belonging to them are to be always in plural. The
nouns אָדוֹן and בַּעַל often come to stand in plural, whilst the
verb and adjective stand in singular, as אֲדֹנִים קָשֶׁה a cruel
lord (Is. xix. 4), וְלֻקַּח בְּעָלָיו.

---

§ XX.—PRONOUNS.

1. The personal pronouns in Hebrew are either separable
words, or letters added to the verb (See § IX. 1). But
sometimes they are both used together, as אָנֹכִי אֶשָּׁבַע,
כַּרְמִי שֶׁלִּי, וְאַתָּה אָמַרְתָּ my own vineyard.

2. Often. the pronouns, in such a case, are changed, e. g.,
יְהוּדָה אַתָּה יוֹדוּךָ אַחֶיךָ Judah, thy brethren shall praise
thee (Gen. xlix. 8), where it ought to be אוֹתְךָ יוֹדוּךְ, or
וּפִגְרֵיכֶם אַתֶּם And your carcases (Numb. xiv. 32), where it
should be וּפִגְרֵיכֶם שֶׁלָּכֶם. Sometimes they stand even
double, e. g., וְהִיא נַם הִיא אָמְרָה And she, even she said
(Gen. xx. 5), הֵם הֵם גּוֹרָלֵךְ they, they are thy lot (Is. lvii.
6), for emphasis' sake.

3. The personal pronoun dative לִי, לְךָ. etc., is sometimes
used without denoting the dative case, as אָשׁוּבָה לִּי I will
return (Numb. xxii. 34). אִם לֹא תֵדְעִי לָךְ · · · · · צְאִי לָךְ

---

* I give it according to the general idea of the Hebrew Grammarians, but I
believe that the nouns מִם, חַיִּים and שָׁמַיִם are rather in Dual form, and that
for certain reason. Of מַיִם we read (Gen. i. 7) that it was divided into two
parts. Of חַיִּים we know that it is divided into two parts, viz., the life here and
hereafter. Also שָׁמַיִם which means sky, and is derived from שָׁם there, space,
is in dual, meaning the two hemispheres. The Kabbala says: אֵין סוֹף בַּד סָלִיק
בִּרְעוּתֵהּ לְאַחֲוְיָה שְׁלֵימוּתֵהּ וּלְאֵיטָבָא בֵהּ פָּנָה אֲתַר When the Infinite intended to
shew his perfection, and to do good by it, he made a place, etc. The place
must be in existence, before anything existing can be. Hence " In the beginning God created heaven, i. e., space, and the earth."

If thou knowest not......go (Cant. i. 8). Yet even here,
where the particle seems to be superfluous, it denotes that the
action is to the advantage of the subject.

4. The demonstrative pronoun זֶה m., זֹאת f., אֵלֶּה pl. c.,
denotes some person or thing which is present, or by relation
we have become aquainted with it, as if it were present, as
אֶל הַנַּעַר הַזֶּה הִתְפַּלָּלְתִּי for this child I prayed (Sam.
i. 27), זֹאת מָצָאנוּ this we found (Gen. xxxvii. 32). The
pron. הַלָּזֶה, הַלָּז are used for a present object at a distance:
מִי הָאִישׁ הַלָּזֶה Who is *that* man? (Gen. xxiv. 65). The
demonstrative זֶה generally stands for concrete nouns, זֹאת
for abstract nouns.

5. Also with these pronouns, as with the verbs, there is a
repetition, when they are connected by the copulative ו, which
denotes a diversity, as זֶה אוֹמֵר בְּכֹה וְזֶה אוֹמֵר בְּכֹה: One
said on this manner, and another said on that manner (1 Kings
xxii. 20). Also אֵלֶּה בָרֶכֶב וְאֵלֶּה בַסּוּסִים These in chariots,
and those in horses (Ps. xx. 8). The personal pronoun is also
sometimes used as a *demonstrative*, as הוּא מֹשֶׁה וְאַהֲרֹן These
are Moses and Aaron (Exodus vi. 27). We often also find
the personal and demonstrative pronouns together, or two
demonstratives (but in which case the second is always הוּא
or הֵם) together, as אָנֹכִי אָנֹכִי הוּא מֹחֶה פְשָׁעֶיךָ I, even
I, am he that blotteth out thy transgressions (Is. xliii. 25).
אֵלֶּה הֵם מוֹעֲדַי These are my feasts (Lev. xxiii. 2). The
second pronoun in these cases is always explanatory of the first.

6. The demonstrative pronouns must also agree with the
noun constructed, like the adjective (See § XVIII. 1). When,
however, the noun to which it is constructed, is the chief noun,
the demonstrative agrees with it, and not with the construct,
as בְּסֵפֶר הַתּוֹרָה הַזֹּאת In the book of this law (Deut. xxviii.
61). The demonstrative can also take a preposition when a
noun is implied by it, as בָזֶה in this place (Gen. xlviii. 9).

Also (Ps. xxvii. 3) בְּזֹאת אֲנִי בוֹטֵחַ In this will I be confident; כַּדָּבָר הַזֹּאת is to be understood.

---

§ XXI.—RELATION OF THE VERB.

1. The verb usually precedes the noun, וַיֹּאמֶר מֹשֶׁה And said Moses. When, however, the emphasis, or stress, is put on the noun, it will precede the verb, as וְשָׂרָה שׁוֹמַעַת And Sarah was hearing (Gen. xviii. 10), וּפַרְעֹה הִקְרִיב And Pharaoh drew nigh (Exod. xiv. 10). When two verbs refer to one noun, the noun stands between the verbs, as וַיֶּאֱהַל אַבְרָם וַיֵּשֶׁב And Abram removed his tent.... and dwelt (Gen. xiii. 18). Where several verbs refer to one noun, the noun stands either after the first or after the last verb.

2. In Hebrew, like in most ancient languages, the second person is addressed in sing. only; if the word *Lord* is added, the verb is put in 3d pers. sing., as אֲדֹנִי שָׁאַל My lord has asked (Gen. xliv. 19), יֵרֶא פַרְעֹה Let Pharaoh look out (ibid. xli. 33). The word אָדֹן or מֶלֶךְ is here to be understood.

3. The verb has three *tenses* (See § X. 5), past, progressive present, and future. The past may imply imperfect, as (Gen. xxi. 1): וַה' פָּקַד אֶת־שָׂרָה And God visited Sarah. Again פָּקַד עֲוֹנֵךְ בַּת אֱדוֹם He has visited thine iniquity, O daughter of Edom (Lam. iv. 22)—and pluperfect, when it follows a perfect, as כִּי שָׁמְעָה······כִּי־פָקַד For she heard......that he had visited (Ruth i. 6). In prophetic language, the past is used for the future, as לְזַרְעֲךָ נָתַתִּי instead of לְזַרְעֲךָ אֶתֵּן (Gen. xv. 18). Thus it is sometimes used for the present, as וְאַתֶּנָה יוֹדְעוֹת for וְאַתֶּנָה יְדַעְתֶּן.

4. The Hebrew language, properly speaking, has no present tense (and in fact, time being transient, cannot have a present). It combines, however, past and future, and forms a present, as

הִנֵּה אָנֹכִי הוֹלֵךְ לָמוּת Behold! I am going (all the time) to die (Gen. xxv. 32). This tense is formed by the participle with the personal pron. nom. before it.

5. This form sometimes also stands for the future, as הִנְנִי מֵבִיא Behold, I shall bring (Gen. vi. 17). Also when an action appears as present, it is used in this form, as וּפַרְעֹה חֹלֵם And Pharaoh was dreaming (Gen. xlviii. 1). When an action which is often repeated is described, the future is used instead of the past, as כָּכָה יַעֲשֶׂה אִיֹּוב So used Job to do (Job i. 5). The same is the case with an action which is entirely independent of time, as בֵּן חָכָם יְשַׂמַּח אָב A wise son makes glad a father (Prov. x. 1).

6. The *Infinitive* gives an abstract idea of the action, as הָלוֹךְ to go, הַכּוֹת to smite; independent of time and person But it may take the prepositions מ, כ, ל, ב, as בַּהֲלוֹךְ in going, כַּהֲלוֹךְ like going, לַהֲלוֹךְ to go (*i. e.*, in order to go), מֵהֲלוֹךְ from going. It is treated like a noun. It is also placed before the past or future to imply a certainty, as פָּקֹד יִפְקֹד he will surely visit (Gen. l. 24). When the *infinitive* is joined to the *imperative* or participle, it takes the second place, as שִׁמְעוּ שָׁמוֹעַ Hear ye indeed! (Is. vi. 9), הוֹלְכִים הָלוֹךְ Still went on (2 Kings ii. 11).

7. The *infinitive Kal*, which is the easiest to be pronounced, is, when in itself without meaning, as above, placed before any other *paradigm* of the same verb, as טָרֹף טֹרַף where the first is in Kal, the second in Pual; גָּנֹב יִגָּנֵב the first Kal, the second Niphal; קַטֵּר יַקְטִירוּן is the first in Piël (but as it is not used in Kal, the Piël stands for Kal) and the second in Hiphil. As the *infinitive* is to be regarded as an abstract noun, it is sometimes interchanged with the participle, as וּמִסְפָּר אֶת רֹבַע יִשְׂרָאֵל And number a fourth part of

Israel (Num. xxiii. 10), instead of קָנֹה חָכְמָה ,וְלִסְפּוֹר for קִנְיַן חָכְמָה

8. The *imperative* mood (See § X. 4) can only be used in the affirmative command; when in the negative, the future with the adverb לֹא or אַל is used, as לֹא תִזְכְּרוּ remember not, אַל תֵּלַכְנָה do not go! etc. The *imperative* also can only be used in *active*, not in *passive* voice; but in Niphal, which is properly a deponent verb and has the same meaning as Kal, the *imperative* is used.

9. The *future* proper has one form (See Tab. of the verb). The Hebrew uses, however, a commanding *future* (jussive) and that by omitting the quiescent letter of the *future* * (apocap.), and a future *optative*, which expresses a wish. The commanding form, as יַמְטֵר he shall (not will) rain (Psalm xi. 6), יְהִי it shall be; or, let there be! is of frequent occurrence. The future *optative* is formed by suffixing ה to the first pers. sing. and pl., and a ן to the second and third pers. plural masc. אֵלְכָה I will go, נֵלְכָה we will go, יֵלְכוּן they will go, תֵּלְכוּן you will go.

---

§ XXII.—VAV CONJUNCTIVE.

1. The letter ו at the beginning of a word (except eleven words, most of which are proper nouns) with a Sh'va (־ְ) used before a letter with a Sh'va, or a letter of its own class ב, מ, פ, is the equivalent of the conjunction *and*.

2. The copulative, by *way of explanation*, as בְּרָמָה וּבְעִירוֹ in Ramah, even in his own city (1 Sam. xxviii. 3). So עִיר וְקָדִישׁ a watcher (*i. e.*, an angel) even a holy one (Dan. iv. 10).

3. As an adversative—*but*—like the adverb אֲבָל as לֹא אֲדֹנִי וַעֲבָדֶיךָ Not so, my lord, but thy servants (Gen. xlii. 10).

---

* Hence this *future* is found in the regular verb in Hiphil, and in verbs ל״ה in all the paradigms.

4. As an apodosis *thou*, as וְצָמִת וְהָלַכְתְּ אֶל הַכֵּלִים And when thou art athirst, then go to the vessels (Ruth ii. 9). The like adverb is אָן or אֲזַי.

5. As the adverb אַף גַּם although, *yet*, as כִּי אֶת־חַנָּה אָהַב וַיי׳ סָגַר רַחְמָהּ For he loved Hannah, yet the Lord had shut up her womb (1 Sam. i. 6).

6. As *adæquationis*, *so*, *just so*, adverb כֵּן, As מַיִם קָרִים עַל נֶפֶשׁ עֲיֵפָה וּשְׁמוּעָה טוֹבָה מֵאֶרֶץ מֶרְחָק As cold water to a thirsty soul, so is good news from a far country (Proverb xxv. 25).

7. As a *disjunctive* (See § XVII. 1), *e. g.*, וּמַכֵּה אָבִיו וְאִמּוֹ And he that smites his father, or his mother (Exod. xxi. 15), like adverb אוֹ.

8. As *inferential*, like the adverb לְמַעַן in order that, as לֹא יַרְבֶּה לּוֹ סוּסִים וְלֹא יָשִׁיב He shall not multiply to himself horses, *that* he cause to return, etc. (Deut. xvii. 16). When doubled וְ‧‧‧‧וְ it signifies *both*.‧‧‧*and*, as וְלַגֵּר וּלְאֶזְרָח·

9. As *conclusive*, like the adverb לָכֵן therefore, as יַעַן מָאַסְתָּ אֶת־דְּבַר י״י וַיִּמְאָסְךָ מִמֶּלֶךְ Because thou hast rejected the word of God, therefore God has rejected thee from being king (1. Sam. xv. 23).

10. As וְ conversive, viz., when וְ with a Sh'va (וְ) is prefixed to the past tense, it means the future, and when a וַ with a Pathach or a Komats (וַ, וָ), is prefixed to the future it denotes the past, as וְאָמַר and he will say, וַיֹּאמֶר and he said. This holds good only in the *narrative* style ; but not otherwise, as וְיִפָּקֵד and he shall appoint (Esther ii. 3).

NOTE.—The root of the Hebrew Verb, consisting of three radicals, being found, without any prefix or suffix, in the 3d person masculine singular of the past tense, the conjugation of the verb therefore begins with the 3d pers. masc. sing. of that tense.

TABLE I.—FIRST PARADIGM פָּעַל OR קַל.

Femin.	Com.	Masc.	
לָמְדָה		לָמַד	3. sing.
לָמַדְתְּ		לָמַדְתָּ	2.
	לָמַדְתִּי		1.
	לָמְדוּ		3. pl.
לְמַדְתֶּן		לְמַדְתֶּם	2.
	לָמַדְנוּ		1.

PARTICIPLE PRESENT ACTIVE.

לוֹמֶדֶת { אָנֹכִי / אַתְּ / הִיא	לוֹמֵד { אָנֹכִי / אַתָּה / הוּא	1. sing. / 2. / 3.
לוֹמְדוֹת { אֲנַחְנוּ / אַתֶּן / הֵן	לוֹמְדִים { אֲנַחְנוּ / אַתֶּם / הֵם	1. pl. / 2. / 3.

PARTICIPLE PRESENT PASSIVE.

Femin.	Masc.	
לְמוּדָה { אָנֹכִי / אַתְּ / הִיא	לָמוּד { אָנֹכִי / אַתָּה / הוּא	1. sing. / 2. / 3.
לְמוּדוֹת { אֲנַחְנוּ / אַתֶּן / הֵן	לְמוּדִים { אֲנַחְנוּ / אַתֶּם / הֵם	1. pl. / 2. / 3.

FUTURE TENSE.

Fem.	Com.	Masc.	
	אֶלְמוֹד		1. sing
תִּלְמְדִי		תִּלְמוֹד	2.
תִּלְמוֹד		יִלְמוֹד	3.
	נִלְמוֹד		1. pl.
תִּלְמוֹדְנָה		תִּלְמְדוּ	2.
תִּלְמוֹדְנָה		יִלְמְדוּ	3.

FUTURE OPTATIVE.

Fem.	Com.	Masc.	
	אֶלְמְדָה		1. sing.
תִּלְמְדִי		תִּלְמוֹד	2.
תִּלְמוֹד		יִלְמוֹד	3.
	נִלְמְדָה		1. pl.
תִּלְמוֹדְנָה		תִּלְמְדוּן	2.
תִּלְמוֹדְנָה		יִלְמְדוּן	3.

INFINITIVE.

	לָמוֹד	abs.
מִלְמוֹד , לִלְמוֹד , כְּלְמוֹד , בִּלְמוֹד , לְמוֹד		cons.

IMPERATIVE.

Fem.	Masc.	
לִמְדִי	לְמוֹד	2. sing.
לִמְדְנָה	לִמְדוּ	2. pl.

PARADIGM נִפְעַל.

Past.

Fem.	Com.	Masc.	
	נִלְמַדְתִּי		1. sing.
נִלְמַדְתְּ		נִלְמַדְתָּ	2.
נִלְמְדָה		נִלְמַד	3.
	נִלְמַדְנוּ		1. pl.
נִלְמַדְתֶּן		נִלְמַדְתֶּם	2.
	נִלְמְדוּ		3.

Participle Passive.

	Fem.			Masc.	
נִלְמָדָה	אָנֹכִי		נִלְמָד	אָנֹכִי	1. sing.
	אַתְּ			אַתָּה	2.
	הִיא			הוּא	3.
נִלְמָדוֹת	אֲנַחְנוּ		נִלְמָדִים	אֲנַחְנוּ	1. pl.
	אַתֶּן			אַתֶּם	2.
	הֵן			הֵם	3.

Future Tense.

Fem.	Com.	Masc.	
	אֶלָּמֵד		1. sing.
תִּלָּמְדִי		תִּלָּמֵד	2.
תִּלָּמֵד		יִלָּמֵד	3.
	נִלָּמֵד		1. pl.
תִּלָּמֵדְנָה		תִּלָּמְדוּ	2.
תִּלָּמֵדְנָה		יִלָּמְדוּ	3.

43

INFINITIVE.

הִלָּמוֹד abs.

מֵהִלָּמֵד , לְהִלָּמֵד , כְּהִלָּמֵד , בְּהִלָּמֵד , הִלָּמֵד con.

IMPERATIVE.

Fem.	Masc.	
הִלָּמְדִי	הִלָּמֵד	2. sing.
הִלָּמֵדְנָה	הִלָּמְדוּ	2. pl.

PARADIGM פֻּעַל.

Past.

Fem.	Com.	Masc.	
	לֻמַּדְתִּי		1. sing.
לֻמַּדְתְּ		לֻמַּדְתָּ	2.
לֻמְּדָה		לֻמַּד	3.
	לֻמַּדְנוּ		1. pl.
לֻמַּדְתֶּן		לֻמַּדְתֶּם	2.
	לֻמְּדוּ		3.

PARTICIPLE ACTIVE.

Fem.		Masc.		
מְלַמֶּדֶת	אָנֹכִי / אַתְּ / הִיא	מְלַמֵּד	אָנֹכִי / אַתָּה / הוּא	1. sing. / 2. / 3.
מְלַמְּדוֹת	אֲנַחְנוּ / אַתֶּן / הֵן	מְלַמְּדִים	אֲנַחְנוּ / אַתֶּם / הֵם	1. pl. / 2. / 3.

FUTURE TENSE.

Fem.	Com.	Masc.	
	אֶלְמַד		1. sing.
תִּלְמְדִי		תִּלְמַד	2.
תִּלְמַד		יִלְמַד	3.
	נִלְמַד		1. pl.
תִּלְמַדְנָה		תִּלְמְדוּ	2.
תִּלְמַדְנָה		יִלְמְדוּ	3.

INFINITIVE.

	לָמֹד	abs.
מִלְמֹד, לִלְמֹד, כִּלְמֹד, בִּלְמֹד,	לְמֹד	con.

IMPERATIVE.

Fem.		Masc.	
לִמְדִי		לְמַד	sing.
לְמַדְנָה		לִמְדוּ	pl.

PARADIGM פְּעַל.

PAST.

Fem.	Com.	Masc.	
	לְמַדְתִּי		1. sing.
לְמַדְתְּ		לְמַדְתָּ	2.
לְמְדָה		לְמַד	3.
	לְמַדְנוּ		1. pl.
לְמַדְתֶּן		לְמַדְתֶּם	2.
	לְמְדוּ		3.

PARTICIPLE PASSIVE.

מְלֻמֶּדֶת	אָנֹכִי	מְלֻמָּד	אָנֹכִי	1. sing.
	אַתְּ		אַתָּה	2.
	הִיא		הוּא	3.
מְלֻמָּדוֹת	אֲנַחְנוּ	מְלֻמָּדִים	אֲנַחְנוּ	1. pl.
	אַתֶּן		אַתֶּם	2.
	הֵן		הֵם	3.

INFINITIVE.

			לַמֹּד	abs.
מְלַמֵּד , לְלַמֵּד , כְּלַמֵּד , בְּלַמֵּד ,			לַמֵּד	con.

No IMPERATIVE.

PARADIGM הִפְעִיל.

PAST.

Fem.	Com.	Masc.	
	הִלְמַדְתִּי		1. sing.
הִלְמַדְתְּ		הִלְמַדְתָּ	2.
הִלְמִידָה		הִלְמִיד	3.
	הִלְמַדְנוּ		1. pl.
הִלְמַדְתֶּן		הִלְמַדְתֶּם	2.
	הִלְמִידוּ		3.

PARTICIPLE ACTIVE.

מַלְמֶדֶת	אָנֹכִי	מַלְמִיד	אָנֹכִי	1. sing.
	אַתְּ		אַתָּה	2.
	הִיא		הוּא	3.
מַלְמִידוֹת	אֲנַחְנוּ	מַלְמִידִים	אֲנַחְנוּ	1. pl.
	אַתֶּן		אַתֶּם	2.
	הֵן		הֵם	3.

Future.

Fem.	Com.	Masc.	
	אֶלְמִיד		1. sing.
תַּלְמִידִי		תַּלְמִיד	2.
תַּלְמִיד		יַלְמִיד	3.
	נַלְמִיד		1. pl.
תַּלְמֵדְנָה		תַּלְמִידוּ	2.
תְּלַמֵדְנָה		יַלְמִידוּ	3.

Future Apocap. (Jussive).

Fem.	Com.	Masc.	
	אַלְמֵד		1. sing.
תַּלְמֵד		תַּלְמֵד	2.
תַּלְמֵד		יַלְמֵד	3.
	נַלְמֵד		1. pl.
תַּלְמֵדְנָה		תַּלְמֵדוּ	2.
תַּלְמֵדְנָה		יַלְמֵדוּ	3.

Infinitive.

הַלְמֵד	abs.
הַלְמִיד , כְּהַלְמִיד , כְּהַלְמִיד , לְהַלְמִיד , מֵהַלְמִיד	con.

Imperative.

Fem.	Masc.	
הַלְמִידִי	הַלְמֵד	2. sing.
הַלְמַדְנָה	הַלְמִידוּ	2. pl.

הָפְעַל PARADIGM.

PAST.

Fem.	Com.	Masc.	
	הָלְמַדְתִּי		1. sing.
הָלְמַדְתְּ		הָלְמַדְתָּ	2.
הָלְמְדָה		הָלְמַד	3.
	הָלְמַדְנוּ		1. pl.
הָלְמַדְתֶּן		הָלְמַדְתֶּם	2.
	הָלְמְדוּ		3.

PARTICIPLE PASSIVE.

PRESENT.

Fem.		Com.	Masc.		
מֶלְמָדָה	אָנֹכִי אַתְּ הִיא		מֶלְמָד	אָנֹכִי אַתָּה הוּא	1. sing. 2. 3.
מֶלְמָדוֹת	אֲנַחְנוּ אַתֶּן הֵן		מֶלְמָדִים	אֲנַחְנוּ אַתֶּם הֵם	1. pl. 2. 3.

FUTURE.

Fem.	Com.	Masc.	
	אָלְמַד		1. sing.
תָּלְמְדִי		תָּלְמַד	2.
תָּלְמַד		יָלְמַד	3.
	נָלְמַד		1. pl.
תָּלְמַדְנָה		תָּלְמְדוּ	2.
תָּלְמַדְנָה		יָלְמְדוּ	3.

INFINITIVE.

הָלְמֵד , בְּהָלְמֵד , כְּהָלְמֵד , לְהָלְמֵד , מֵהָלְמֵד

No IMPERATIVE.

PARADIGM הִתְפַּעֵל.

PAST.

Fem.	Com.	Masc.	
	הִתְלַמַּדְתִּי		1. sing.
הִתְלַמַּדְתְּ		הִתְלַמַּדְתָּ	2.
הִתְלַמְּדָה		הִתְלַמֵּד	3.
	הִתְלַמַּדְנוּ		1. pl.
הִתְלַמַּדְתֶּן		הִתְלַמַּדְתֶּם	2.
	הִתְלַמְּדוּ		3.

PARTICIPLE.

מִתְלַמֶּדֶת	אָנֹכִי		מִתְלַמֵּד	אָנֹכִי		1. sing.
	אַתְּ			אַתָּה		2.
	הִיא			הוּא		3.
מִתְלַמְּדוֹת	אֲנַחְנוּ		מִתְלַמְּדִים	אֲנַחְנוּ		1. pl.
	אַתֶּן			אַתֶּם		2.
	הֵן			הֵם		3.

FUTURE.

Fem.	Com.	Masc.	
	אֶתְלַמֵּד		1. sing.
תִּתְלַמְּדִי		תִּתְלַמֵּד	2.
תִּתְלַמֵּד		יִתְלַמֵּד	3.
	נִתְלַמֵּד		1. pl.
תִּתְלַמֵּדְנָה		תִּתְלַמְּדוּ	2.
תִּתְלַמֵּדְנָה		יִתְלַמְּדוּ	3.

INFINITIVE.

הִתְלַמֵּד

מֵהִתְלַמֵּד , לְהִתְלַמֵּד , כְּהִתְלַמֵּד , בְּהִתְלַמֵּד

IMPERATIVE.

Fem.	Masc.	
הִתְלַמְּדִי	הִתְלַמֵּד	2. sing.
הִתְלַמֵּדְנָה	הִתְלַמְּדוּ	2. pl.

Only the Preterit of קַל have I put according to the general Hebrew Tables, 3d pers. masc. sing. first. In the rest of Paradigms the order of the persons and tenses is according to the modern languages.

——— • ◆ • ———

The following Table is a Paradigm of Kal קַל with Pronominal Suffixes, which serves also for the entire verb, as they are affixed in a similar manner to the remaining Conjugations whose meaning admits of their reception, with the exception of Piël פִּעֵל which slightly deviates.

———

VERB קַל WITH AFFIXES.

PRETERITE OF לָמַד "he taught."

לְמָדָנוּ	1. c. pl. suffix.	לְמָדָנִי	1. c. sing. suffix.
לְמַדְכֶם	2. m.	לְמָדְךָ	2. m.
לְמַ־דְכֶן	2. f.	לְמָדֵךְ	2. f.
לְמָדָם	3. m.	לְמָדוּ / לְמָדָהוּ	3. m.
לְמָדָן	3. f.	לְמָדָהּ	3. f.

לִמְּדָה "she taught."

לִמְּדַתְנוּ	1. c. pl. suffix.	לִמְּדַתְנִי		1. c. sing. suffix.
לִמֶּדְתְכֶם	2. m.	לִמֶּדְתְךָ		2. m.
לִמְּדַתְכֶן	2. f.	לִמְּדָתֶךְ		2. f.
		לִמְּדַתּוּ	} 3. m.	
לִמְּדָתַם	3. m.	לִמְּדַתְהוּ		
		לִמְּדַתָּהּ	} 3. f.	
לִמְּדָתַן	3. f.	לִמְּדַתָּהּ		

לִמַּדְתָ "thou didst teach."

לִמַּדְתָּנוּ	1. c. pl. suffix.	לִמַּדְתָּנִי		1. c. sing. suffix.
לִמַּדְתָּם	} 3. m.	לִמַּדְתּוֹ	} 3. m.	
לִמַּדְתָּמוֹ		לִמַּדְתָּהוּ		
לִמַּדְתָּן	3. f.	לִמַּדְתָּהּ		3. f.

לִמַּדְתְ "thou (f.) didst teach."

לִמַּדְתִּינוּ	1. c. pl. suffix.	לִמַּדְתִּינִי	1. c. sing. suffix.
לִמַּדְתִּים	3. m.	לִמַּדְתִּיהוּ	3. m.
לִמַּדְתִּין	3. f.	לִמַּדְתִּיהָ	3. f.

לִמַּדְתִּי "I taught."

לִמַּדְתִּיכֶם	2. m. pl. suffix.	לִמַּדְתִּיךָ		2. m. sing. suffix.
לִמַּדְתִּיכֶן	2. f.	לִמַּדְתִּיךְ		2. f.
		לִמַּדְתִּיו	} 3. m.	
לִמַּדְתִּים	3. m.	לִמַּדְתִּיהוּ		
לִמַּדְתִּין	3. f.	לִמַּדְתִּיהָ		3. f.

לָמְדוּ "they taught."

לִמְּדוּנוּ	1. c. pl. suffix.	לִמְּדוּנִי	1. c. sing. suffix.
לִמְּדוּכֶם	2. m.	לִמְּדוּךָ	2. m.
לִמְּדוּכֶן	2. f.	לִמְּדוּךְ	2. f.
לִמְּדוּם	3. m.	לִמְּדוּהוּ	3. m.
לִמְּדוּן	3. f.	לִמְּדוּהָ	3. f.

___

לִמַּדְתֶּם or לִמַּדְתֶּן "ye did teach."

לִמַּדְתּוּנוּ	1. c. pl. suffix.	לִמַּדְתּוּנִי	1. c. sing. suffix.
לִמַּדְתּוּם	3. m.	לִמַּדְתּוּהוּ	3. m.
לִמַּדְתּוּן	3. f.	לִמַּדְתּוּהָ	3. f.

___

לָמַדְנוּ "we did learn."

לְמַדְנוּכֶם	2. m. pl. suffix.	לְמַדְנוּךָ	2. m. sing. suffix.
לְמַדְנוּכֶן	2. f.	לְמַדְנוּךְ	2. f.
לְמַדְנוּם	3. m.	לְמַדְנוּהוּ	3. m.
לְמַדְנוּן	3. f.	לְמַדְנוּהָ	3. f.

___

Participle act. לוֹמֵד learning, or a learner, is suffixed like the noun. Likewise the participle passive לָמוּד.

___

Future, יִלְמוֹד "he will learn."

יִלְמְדֵנוּ	1. c. pl. suffix.	יִלְמְדֵנִי	1. c. sing. suffix.
יִלְמָדְכֶם	2. m.	יִלְמָדְךָ	2. m.
יִלְמָדְכֶן	2. f.	יִלְמָדֵךְ	2. f.
יִלְמָדֵם	3. m.	יִלְמָדֵהוּ	3. m.
יִלְמָדֵן	3. f.	יִלְמָדֶהָ	3. f.

The 1st sing. and pl. and 2d m. sing. follow the same form, by changing (וֹ) into (—ָ); but before the suffixes כֶן, כֶם, and ךָ it is changed into short (—ַ). ךָ is preceded by (ֵ‍).

The 2d fem. sing. and 3d and 2d pl. m. take the suffixes without any change. The 2d and 3d pl. f. drop נָה and preceding וֹ.

INFINITIVE לְמוֹד "to learn."

לְמָדְנוּ	1. c. pl. suffix.	לְמָדִי	1. c. sing. suffix.
לְמָדְכֶם	2. m.	לְמָדְךָ	2. m.
לְמָדְכֶן	2. f.	לְמָדֵךְ	2. f.
לְמָדֵם	3. m.	לְמָדוֹ	3. m.
לְמָדֵן	3. f.	לְמָדָהּ	3. f.

IMPERATIVE לְמֹד "learn!"

לְמָדֵנוּ	1. c. pl. suffix.	לְמָדֵנִי	1. c. sing. suffix.
לְמָדֵם	3. m.	לְמָדֵהוּ	3. m.
לְמָדֵן	3. f.	לְמָדֵהּ	3. f.

PARADIGM פָּעַל WITH SUFFIXES.

לִמְדַנוּ	1. c. pl. suffix.	לִמְדַנִי	1. c. sing. suffix.
לִמְדְכֶם	2. m.	לִמְדְךָ	2. m.
לִמְדְכֶן	2. f.	לִמְדֵךְ	2. f.
לִמְדָם	3. m.	לִמְדוֹ	3. m.
לִמְדָן	3. f.	לִמְדָהּ	3. f.

TABLE II.—VERB א״פ QUIESCENT.

	קל	נפעל	פעל	פֻעל	הפעיל	הֻפעל	התפעל
Past Tense.	אָכַל	נֶאֱכַל	אִכֵּל	אֻכַּל	הֶאֱכִיל	הָאֳכַל	הִתְאַכֵּל
Part. Act.	אֹכֵל		מְאַכֵּל		מַאֲכִיל		מִתְאַכֵּל
Part. Pass.	אָכוּל	נֶאֱכָל		מְאֻכָּל		מָאֳכָל	
Future.	יֹאכַל	יֵאָכֵל	יְאַכֵּל	יְאֻכַּל	יַאֲכִיל	יָאֳכַל	יִתְאַכֵּל
Fut. Apo.							
Infin. abs.	אָכוֹל	נֶאֱכֹל	אַכֵּל		הַאֲכֵל	הָאֳכֵל	הִתְאַכֵּל
Infin. con.	אֱכֹל	הֵאָכֵל	אַכֵּל		הַאֲכִיל		
Imperative.	אֱכֹל	הֵאָכֵל	אַכֵּל		הַאֲכֵל		
Fut. optat.					נַאֲכִילָה		

LIBRARY UNIVERSITY CALIFORNIA

TABLE III.—VERB פ״נ IMPERFECT (§ XI. 1).

PARADIGM קַל.

Past.

Fem.	Com.	Masc.	
נָגְשָׁה		נָגַשׁ	3. sing.
נָגַשְׁתְּ		נָגַשְׁתָּ	2.
	נָגַשְׁתִּי		1.
	נָגְשׁוּ		3. pl.
נְגַשְׁתֶּן		נְגַשְׁתֶּם	2.
	נָגַשְׁנוּ		1.

Participle Active (Progressive Present).

Fem.		Masc.		
נוֹגֶשֶׁת {	אֲנִי / אַתְּ / הִיא	נוֹגֵשׁ {	אֲנִי / אַתָּה / הוּא	1. sing. / 2. / 3.
נגְשׁוֹת {	אֲנַחְנוּ / אַתֶּן / הֵן	נגְשִׁים {	אֲנַחְנוּ / אַתֶּם / הֵם	1. pl. / 2. / 3.

Participle Passive Regular.

Future.

Fem.	Com.	Masc.	
	אֶגַּשׁ		1. sing.
תִּגְּשִׁי		תִּגַּשׁ	2.
תִּגַּשׁ		יִגַּשׁ	3.
	נִגַּשׁ		1. pl.
תִּגַּשְׁנָה		תִּגְּשׁוּ	2.
תִּגַּשְׁנָה		יִגְּשׁוּ	3.

INFINITIVE.

		נָגוֹשׁ	abs.
מִגֶּשֶׁת , לָגֶשֶׁת , כְּגֶשֶׁת , בִּגֶשֶׁת ,		גֶּשֶׁת	con.

IMPERATIVE.

Fem.	Masc.	
גְּשִׁי	גַּשׁ	2. sing.
גַּשְׁנָה	גְּשׁוּ	2. pl.

PARADIGM נִפְעַל.

PAST.

Fem.	Com.	Masc.	
נִגְּשָׁה		נִגַּשׁ	3. sing.
נִגַּשְׁתְּ		נִגַּשְׁתָּ	2.
	נִגַּשְׁתִּי		1.
	נִגְּשׁוּ		3. pl.
נִגַּשְׁתֶּן		נִגַּשְׁתֶּם	2.
	נִגַּשְׁנוּ		1.

PARTICIPLE PASSIVE.

נִגָּשׁ		
נָגוֹשׁ , הִנָּגשׁ	abs.	
הַנָּגֹשׁ etc.	con.	

The conjugation of the rest of Niphal is regular. Fut. יִנָּגֵשׁ.
Piël and Pual like the regular verb.

PARADIGM הִפְעִיל.

Past Tense	הִגִּישׁ etc.	Future Apoc.	יַגֵּשׁ etc.
Participle	מַגִּישׁ etc.	Infinitive, abs. הַגֵּשׁ, con. הַגִּישׁ etc.	
Future simple	יַגִּישׁ etc.	Imperative	הַגֵּשׁ etc.
Future optative	אַגִּישָׁה etc.		

PARADIGM הִפְעַל.

Past Tense	הֻגַּשׁ	Future Tense	יֻגַּשׁ
Participle	מֻגָּשׁ	Infinitive	הֻגַּשׁ

No Imperative.

The Hithpael is conjugated like the regular verb.

———•—•———

Verbs פ"י are of three classes.

1. Where, when the first radical י is omitted, the second radical takes a daghesh. Of this class there are but four verbs, viz., יָצַע to spread out, fut. וְיַצַע; יָצַק to pour, fut. יִצַק; יָצַר to form, fut. וְיַצַר; and lastly יָצַת to kindle, fut. וְיַצַת.

2. Where the Verb is originally a פ"ו, in which case the first letter is either dropped or changed into ו in some of the paradigms.

3. Were the Verb is originally פ"י, in which case the first letter י is retained throughout all tenses and paradigms.

————

TABLE IV.—VERB IMPERFECT פ"י (Originally פ"ו).

PARADIGM קָל.

Past.

Fem.	Com.	Masc.	
יָשְׁבָה		יָשַׁב	3. sing
יָשַׁבְתְּ		יָשַׁבְתָּ	2.
	יָשַׁבְתִּי		1.
	יָשְׁבוּ		3. pl.
יְשַׁבְתֶּן		יְשַׁבְתֶּם	2.
	יָשַׁבְנוּ		1.

PARTICIPLE ACTIVE (PROGRESSIVE PRES).

	Fem.	Com.	Masc.	
אָנֹכִי			אָנֹכִי	1. sing.
אַתְּ	יוֹשֶׁבֶת	יֹשֵׁב	אַתָּה	2.
הִיא			הוּא	3.
אֲנַחְנוּ			אֲנַחְנוּ	1. pl.
אַתֵּן	יוֹשְׁבוֹת	יוֹשְׁבִים	אַתֶּם	2.
הֵן			הֵם	3.

PARTICIPLE PASSIVE יָשׁוּב "seated,"
is conjugated like the Participle Active.

FUTURE.

Fem.	Com.	Masc.	
	אֵשֵׁב		1. sing.
	optat. אֵשְׁבָה		
תֵּשְׁבִי		תֵּשֵׁב	2.
תֵּשֵׁב		יֵשֵׁב	3.
	נֵשֵׁב		1. pl.
	optat. נֵשְׁבָה		
תֵּשַׁבְנָה		תֵּשְׁבוּ	2.
		opt. תֵּשְׁבוּן	
תֵּשַׁבְנָה		יֵשְׁבוּ	3.
		opt. יֵשְׁבוּן	

INFINITIVE.

יָשׁוּב	abs.
שֶׁבֶת , בְּשֶׁבֶת , כְּשֶׁבֶת , לָשֶׁבֶת , מִשֶּׁבֶת	con.

IMPERATIVE.

Fem.	Masc.	
שְׁבִי	שֵׁב	2. sing.
שֵׁבְנָה	שְׁבוּ	2. pl.

PARADIGM נִפְעַל VERB פ"י (ORIG. פ"ו).

Past Tense נוֹשַׁב, נוֹשְׁבָה etc. | Future Tense יִוָּשֵׁב etc.
Par. Pass. נוֹשָׁב, f. נוֹשֶׁבֶת etc. | Infinitive abs. and con. הִוָּשֵׁב
Imperative, as Infinitive.

PARADIGMS פֻּעַל, פִּעֵל AND הִתְפַּעֵל
are conjugated like the regular Verb.

PARADIGM הִפְעִיל.

Past T. הוֹשִׁיב, הוֹשִׁיבָה etc. | Future Apocap. יוֹשֵׁב etc.
Part. Act. מוֹשִׁיב f. מוֹשֶׁבֶת | Infin. abs. הוֹשֵׁב con. הוֹשִׁיב
Future Tense יוֹשִׁיב etc. | Imperat. הוֹשֵׁב, הוֹשִׁיבִי etc.

PARADIGM הָפְעַל.

PastTense הוּשַׁב, הוּשְׁבָה etc. | Fut. Tense תּוּשַׁב, יוּשַׁב etc.
Part. Pas. מוּשָׁב f. מוּשָׁבָה etc. | Infin. abs. and con. הוּשַׁב etc.
No Imperative.

TABLE V.—VERB PROPER פ"י, יָנַק " to suck."

PAST.

Fem.	Com.	Masc.	
יָנְקָה		יָנַק	3. sing.
יָנַקְתְּ		יָנַקְתָּ	2.
	יָנַקְתִּי		1.
	יָנְקוּ		3. pl.
יְנַקְתֶּן		יְנַקְתֶּם	2.
	יָנַקְנוּ		1.

PARTICIPLE ACTIVE.
PRESENT.

Fem.				Masc.	
	אָנֹכִי			אָנֹכִי	1. sing.
יוֹנֶקֶת	אַתְּ		יוֹנֵק	אַתָּה	2.
	הִיא			הוּא	3.
	אֲנַחְנוּ			אֲנַחְנוּ	1. pl.
יֹנְקוֹת	אַתֵּן		יֹנְקִים	אַתֶּם	2.
	הֵן			הֵם	3.

PARTICIPLE PASSIVE יָנוּק, f. יְנוּקָה
is conjugated like Participle Passive.

FUTURE.

Fem.	Com.	Masc.	
	אִינָק		1. sing.
תִּינְקִי		תִּינָק	2.
תִּינָק		יִינָק	3.
	נִינָק		1. pl.
תִּינַקְנָה		תִּינְקוּ	2.
תִּינָקְנָה		יִנָקוּ	3.

INFINITIVE MOOD.

					יָנוֹק	abs.
מִינָק ,	לִינָק ,	בִּינָק ,	בִּינָק ,	יְנֹק		con.

IMPERATIVE MOOD.

Fem.	Masc.
יִנְקִי	יְנַק
יְנַקְנָה	יִנְקוּ

PARADIGM הִפְעִיל.

Past Tense הֵינִיק, הֵינִיקָה etc.	Future Apoc. יֵינֵק, תֵּינֵק etc.
Part. Act. f. מֵינֶקֶת מֵינִיק etc.	Imp. Mood הֵינִק, הֵינִיקִי etc.
Simple Fut. יֵינִיק, תֵּינִיק etc.	Infinitive Mood הֵינֵק etc.

TABLE VI.—VERB קוּם, ע"ו "to stand."

PAST.

קַל	נִפְעַל	פֻּעַל	פָּעַל	
קָם	נָקוֹם	קוֹמֵם	קוֹמַם	3. m. sing.
קָמָה	נָקוֹמָה	קוֹמְמָה		3. f.
קַמְתָּ	נְקוֹמוֹת	קוֹמַמְתָּ	All the rest like in פִּעֵל	2. m.
קַמְתְּ	נְקוֹמוֹת	קוֹמַמְתְּ		2. f.
קַמְתִּי	נְקוֹמוֹתִי	קוֹמַמְתִּי		1. c.
קָמוּ	נָקוֹמוּ	קוֹמְמוּ		3. c. pl.
קַמְתֶּם	נְקוֹמוֹתֶם	קוֹמַמְתֶּם		2. m.
קַמְתֶּן	נְקוֹמוֹתֶן	קוֹמַמְתֶּן		2. f.
קַמְנוּ	נְקוֹמוֹנוּ	קוֹמַמְנוּ		1. c.
con. abs. קוֹם, קוּם	הִקּוֹם	קוֹמֵם	קוֹמַם	Infinitive.
קוּם	הִקּוֹם	קוֹמֵם	No Imperative.	Imperat.
קוּמִי	הִקּוֹכִי	קוֹמְמִי		
קוּמוּ	הִקּוֹמוּ	קוֹמְמוּ		
קְמְנָה	הִקּוֹמְנָה	קוֹמֵמְנָה		

FUTURE.

Kal.	Niphal.	Piel.	Pual.	
יָקוּם	יִקּוֹם	יְקוֹמֵם	יְקוֹמַם	3. m. sing.
תָּקוּם	תִּקּוֹם	תְּקוֹמֵם	תְּקוֹמַם	3. f.
תָּקוּם	תִּקּוֹם	תְּקוֹמֵם	תְּקוֹמַם	2. m.
תָּקוּמִי	תִּקּוֹמִי	תְּקוֹמְמִי	תְּקוֹמְמִי	2. f.
אָקוּם	אִקּוֹם	אֲקוֹמֵם	אֲקוֹמַם	1. c.
יָקוּמוּ	יִקּוֹמוּ	יְקוֹמְמוּ	יְקוֹמְמוּ	3. m. pl.
תְּקוּמֶינָה	תִּקּוֹמְנָה	תְּקוֹמֵמְנָה	תְּקוֹמַמְנָה	3. f.
תָּקוּמוּ	תִּקּוֹמוּ	תְּקוֹמְמוּ	תְּקוֹמְמוּ	2. m.
תְּקוּמֶינָה	תִּקּוֹמְנָה	תְּקוֹמֵמְנָה	תְּקוֹמַמְנָה	2. f.
נָקוּם	נִקּוֹם	נְקוֹמֵם	נְקוֹמַם	1 c.

Kal.	Niphal.	Piel.	Pual.	
Act. Pass.				
קוּם, קָם	נָקוֹם	מְקוֹמֵם	מְקוֹמָם	Participle

Hiphil.	Hophal.	Hiphil.	Hophal.	
הֵקִים	הוּקַם	הֲקִימוֹתִי	הוּקַמְתִּי	Past T.
הֵקִימָה	הוּקְמָה	הֵקִימוּ	הוּקְמוּ	
הֲקִימוֹתָ	הוּקַמְתָּ	הֲקִימוֹתֶם	הוּקַמְתֶּם	
		ן........	ן........	
הֲקִימוֹת	הוּקַמְתְּ	הֲקִימוֹנוּ	הוּקַמְנוּ	

N B.—The Hithpaël הִתְפָּעֵל of verbs ע״ו are regularly formed by the syllable הִת prefixed to the Paradigm Piel, פֵּעֵל, e. g., קוֹמֵם, הִתְקוֹמֵם, עוֹרֵר, הִתְעוֹרֵר, etc.

TABLE VII.

VERB DOUBLE AYIN ע"ע, סָבַב "to surround"

Kal.		Niphal.	Piel.	Pual.	
2.	**1.**				
סַב ,	סָבַב	נָסַב	סוֹבֵב	סוֹבַב	3. m. sing.
סַבָּה ,	סָבְבָה				3. f.
סַבּוֹתָ ,	סָבַבְתָּ				2. m.
סַבּוֹת ,	סָבַבְתְּ				2. f.
סַבּוֹתִי ,	סָבַבְתִּי	Regular, following No. 2 of Kal	Regularly following verb ע"ע	Regularly like verb ע"ע	1. c.
סַבּוּ ,	סָבְבוּ				3. c. pl.
סַבּוֹתֶם ,	סָבַבְתֶּם				2. m.
סַבּוֹתֶן ,	סָבַבְתֶּן				2. f.
סַבּוֹנוּ ,	סָבַבְנוּ				1. c.

INFINITIVE.

	Kal.	Niphal.	Piel.	Pual.	
absolute	סָבוֹב	הִסּוֹב	סוֹבֵב	סוֹבַב	
construct	סֹב	הִסֵּב			

IMPERATIVE.

	Kal.	Niphal.	Piel.	Pual.	
	סֹב	הִסַּב	סוֹבֵב		2. m. sing.
	סוֹבִּי	הִסַּבִּי	סוֹבְבִי	Is wanting.	2. f.
	סֹבּוּ	הִסַּבּוּ	סוֹבְבוּ		2. m. pl.
	סֻבֶּינָה	הִסֻּבֶּינָה	סוֹבֵבְנָה		2. f.

FUTURE.

	Kal.	Niphal.	Piel.	Pual.	
יָסֹב ,	יִסֹּב	יִסַּב	etc. יְסוֹבֵב	etc. יְסוֹבַב	3. m. sing.
תָּסֹב ,	תִּסֹּב	תִּסַּב			3. f.
תָּסֹב ,	תִּסֹּב	תִּסַּב	like verb ע"ע	like verb ע"ע	2. m.
תָּסֹבִּי ,	תִּסֹּבִּי	תִּסַּבִּי			2. f.
etc. אָסֹב ,	אֶסֹּב	etc. אֶסַּב			1. c.

PARTICIPLE.

Kal.	Niphal.	Piel.	Pual.	
סֹבֵב סָבוּב	נָסָב	מְסוֹבֵב	מְסוֹבָב	active. passive.

Hiphil.	Hophal.	Hithpael.	
הֵסֵב	הוּסַב	הִסְתּוֹבֵב	past.
הָסֵב	הוּסַב	הִסְתּוֹבֵב	infinitive.
הָסֵב	wanting	הִסְתּוֹבֵב	imperat.
יַסֵב , יָסֵב	יְסַב , יוּסַב	יִסְתּוֹבֵב	future.
מֵסֵב		מִסְתּוֹבֵב	partic.
	מוּסָב		

TABLE VIII.—VERB ל״א, מָצָא "he found."

Kal.	Niphal.	Piel.	Pual.	Persons.	
מָצָא	נִמְצָא	מִצָּא	מֻצָּא	3. m. sing.	
מָצְאָה	נִמְצְאָה	מִצְּאָה	מֻצְּאָה	3. f.	
מָצָאתָ	נִמְצֵאתָ	מִצֵּאתָ	מֻצֵּאתָ	2. m.	
מָצָאת	נִמְצֵאת	מִצֵּאת	מֻצֵּאת	2. f.	Past Tense.
מָצָאתִי	נִמְצֵאתִי	מִצֵּאתִי	מֻצֵּאתִי	1. c.	
מָצְאוּ	נִמְצְאוּ	מִצְּאוּ	מֻצְּאוּ	3. c. pl.	
מְצָאתֶם	נִמְצֵאתֶם	מִצֵּאתֶם	מֻצֵּאתֶם	2. m.	
מְצָאתֶן	נִמְצֵאתֶן	מִצֵּאתֶן	מֻצֵּאתֶן	2. f.	
מָצָאנוּ	נִמְצֵאנוּ	מִצֵּאנוּ	מֻצֵּאנוּ	1. c.	
מָצוֹא	נִמְצֹא	מַצֵּא	wanting.	absolute.	Infinit.
מְצֹא	הִמָּצֵא	מַצֵּא		construct.	
מְצָא	הִמָּצֵא	מַצֵּא	wanting.	2. m. sing.	Imperative.
מִצְאִי	etc.	etc.		2. f.	
מִצְאוּ				2. m. pl.	
מְצֶאנָה				2. f.	
יִמְצָא etc.	יִמָּצֵא etc.	יְמַצֵּא etc.	יְמֻצָּא etc.	Future.	
מֹצֵא		מְמַצֵּא		active.	Partic.
מָצוּא	נִמְצָא		מְמֻצָּא	passive.	

LIBRA
UNIVERSIT
CALIFOR

VERB ל״א, מָצָא " he found " (Continued).

Hiphil.	Hophal.	Hithpael.	Persons.	
הִמְצִיא	הֻמְצָא	הִתְמַצֵּא	3. m. sing.	Past Tense.
הִמְצִיאָה	etc.	הִתְמַצְּאָה	3. f.	
הִמְצֵאתָ		הִתְמַצֵּאתָ	2. m.	
הִמְצֵאת		הִתְמַצֵּאת	2. f.	
הִמְצֵאתִי		הִתְמַצֵּאתִי	1. c.	
etc.		הִתְמַצְּאוּ	3. c. pl.	
		הִתְמַצֵּאתֶם	2. m.	
		הִתְמַצֵּאתֶן	2. f.	
		הִתְמַצֵּאנוּ	1. c.	
הַמְצֵא	wanting.	wanting.	absol.	Infinit.
הַמְצִיא	הֻמְצֵה	הִתְמַצֵּא	const.	
הַמְצֵא	wanting.	הִתְמַצֵּא	2. m. sing.	Imperat.
etc.		etc.	2. f.	
			2. m. pl.	
			2. f.	
יַמְצִיא	יֻמְצָא	יִתְמַצֵּא	Future.	
apoc. יַמְצֵא	etc.	etc.		
מַמְצִיא		מִתְמַצֵּא	act.	Partic.
	מֻמְצָא		pass.	

TABLE IX.—VERB גָּלָה, ל"ה "to reveal."

Kal.	Niphal.	Piel.	Pual.	Persons.	
גָּלָה	נִגְלָה	etc. גִּלָּה	etc. גֻּלָּה	3. m. sing.	
גָּלְתָה	נִגְלְתָה			3. f.	
גָּלִיתָ	נִגְלֵיתָ			2. m.	
גָּלִית	נִגְלֵית			2. f.	Past Tense.
גָּלִיתִי	נִגְלֵיתִי			1. c.	
גָּלוּ	נִגְלוּ			3. c. pl.	
גְּלִיתֶם	נִגְלֵיתֶם			2. m.	
גְּלִיתֶן	נִגְלֵיתֶן			2. f.	
גָּלִינוּ	נִגְלֵינוּ			1. c.	
גָּלֹה	נִגְלֹה	גָּלֹה · גַּלֵּה		abs.	Infinit.
גְּלוֹת	הִגָּלוֹת	גַּלּוֹת	גֻּלּוֹת	con.	
etc. גְּלֵה	etc. הִגָּלֵה	etc גַּלֵּה	wanting.	Imperat.	
etc. יִגְלֶה	etc. יִגָּלֶה	etc. יְגַלֶּה	etc. יְגֻלֶּה	Future.	
etc. יִגֶל	etc. יִגָּל	etc. יְגַל		Fut. apoc.	
גֹּלֶה	נִגְלֶה	מְגַלֶּה		act.	Partic.
גָּלוּי	נִגְלֶה		מְגֻלֶּה	pass.	

VERB לָ"ה , גָּלָה "to reveal" (Continued).

Hiphil.	Hophal.	Hithpael.	Persons.	
etc. הִגְלָה	etc. הָגְלָה	etc. הִתְגַּלָּה	3. m. sing.	
			3. f.	
			2. m.	
			2. f.	Past Tense.
			1. c.	
			3. c. pl.	
			2. m.	
			2. f.	
			1. c.	
הַגְלֵה	הָגְלֵה		absol.	Infinit.
הַגְלוֹת	הָגְלוֹת	הִתְגַּלּוֹת	const.	
etc. יַגְלֶה	etc. יָגְלֶה	etc. יִתְגַּלֶּה	Future.	
etc. יַגֵל		etc. יִתְגַּל	Fut. apoc.	
etc. הַגְלֵה	wanting.	etc. הִתְגַּלֵּה	Imperat.	
מַגְלֶה		מִתְגַּלֶּה	act.	Partic.
	מָגְלֶה		pass.	

TABLE X.—SUBSTANTIVE VERB *To be.*

KAL

PRETERIT		FUTURE	
הָיָה	3. m. sing.	יִהְיֶה	3. m. sing.
הָיְתָה	3. fem.	תִּהְיֶה	3. fem.
הָיִיתָ	2. m.	תִּהְיֶה	2. m.
הָיִית	2. fem.	תִּהְיִי	2. fem.
הָיִיתִי	1. com.	אֶהְיֶה	1. com.
הָיוּ	3. com. pl.	יִהְיוּ	3 m. pl.
		תִּהְיֶינָה	3. fem.
הֱיִיתֶם	2. m.	תִּהְיוּ	2. m.
הֱיִיתֶן	2. fem.	תִּהְיֶינָה	2. fem.
הָיִינוּ	1. com.	נִהְיֶה	1. com.

NIFAL

נִהְיָה	3. m. sing.	he is
נִהְיְתָה	3. fem.	she is
נִהְיֵיתָ	2. m.	thou art, m.
נִהְיֵית	2. fem.	thou art, fem.
נִהְיֵיתִי	1. com.	אֶהְיֶה, יֵשׁ I am.
נִהְיוּ	3. com. pl.	they are, m.
נִהְיֶינָה	2. m.	they are, fem.
נִהְיֵיתֶם	2. fem.	you are, m.
נִהְיֵיתֶן	1. com.	you are, fem.
נִהְיֵינוּ		אָנוּ יֵשׁ we are.

Infinitive.

הָיֹה , הָיֹה absol.

הֱיוֹת const.

הֱיוֹתָה

הֱיוֹתֶךָ

הֱיוֹתְךָ

הֱיוֹתְכֶם

Imperative.

הֱיֵה , הְיֵה 2. m. sing.

הֱיִי , הְיִי 2. fem.

הֱיוּ 2. m. pl.

הֱיֶינָה 2. fem.

with ו convers. וַיְהִי

in paus. וַיֶּהִי

Fut. apoc.

יְהִי 3. m. sing.

תְּהִי 3. fem.

תְּהִי 2. m.

תְּהִי 2. fem.

אֱהִי 1. com.

in plur. only

נְהִי 1. com.

Participle

הֹוֶה

Participle.

נִהְיָה

All the other moods and tenses are wanting.

יֶשׁ־לִי I have (there is to me.)

יֶשׁ־לְךָ thou hast. m.

יֶשׁ־לָךְ thou hast, fem.

יֶשׁ־לוֹ he has

יֶשׁ־לָהּ she has

יֶשׁ־לָנוּ we have

יֶשׁ־לָכֶם you have, m.

יֶשׁ־לָכֶן you have, fem.

יֶשׁ־לָהֶם they have, m.

יֶשׁ־לָהֶן they have, f.

הָיָה־לִי I had, liter. it became to me.]

TABLE XI.—VERB IRREGULAR הָלַךְ to go.

	KAL			PIEL			HIFIL		
	m. pret.	com.	fem.	m. pret.	com.	fem.	m. pret.	com.	fem.
3. sing.	הָלַךְ		הָלְכָה	הִלֵּךְ		הִלְּכָה	הִלֵּיךְ		הִלְּכָה
2.	הָלַכְתָּ		הָלַכְתְּ	הִלַּכְתָּ		הִלַּכְתְּ	הִלַּכְתָּ		הִלַּכְתְּ
1.		הָלַכְתִּי			הִלַּכְתִּי			הִלַּכְתִּי	
3. pl.	הָלְכוּ			הִלְּכוּ			הִלְּכוּ		
2.	הֲלַכְתֶּם		הֲלַכְתֶּן	הִלַּכְתֶּם		הִלַּכְתֶּן	הִלַּכְתֶּם		הִלַּכְתֶּן
1.		הָלַכְנוּ			הִלַּכְנוּ			הִלַּכְנוּ	

KAL — infin. abs. הָלוֹךְ — const. לֶכֶת / לְכֶת

PIEL — infin. abso. הַלֵּךְ — const. הַלֵּךְ — with suffix like Kal.

HIFIL — infin. הוֹלֵיךְ

imper. (KAL) — לֵךְ, לְכִי, לְכוּ, לֵכְנָה

imper. (PIEL) — הַלֵּךְ / הַלְּכוּ

imper. (HIFIL) — הוֹלֵךְ / הוֹלִיכוּ

FUTURE.

תִּהָלֵל [יִהָלֵל] יִהָלֵל 3. sing.
תִּהָלֵל תִּהָלֵל 2.
אֶהָלֵל 1. pl.
נֵהָלֵל
יֵהָלְלוּ [יֵהָלְלוּ]‎ 3.
תֵּהָלַלְנָה תֵּהָלְלוּ 2.
נֵהָלֵל 1.

PARTICIPLE ACTIVE.

נֶהְלָל { מָהֳלָל אֵת נֶהֱלַל הוּא
{ אַתְּ אַתָּה נִי

נֶהְלָלֵי { נֶהֳלָלִים אֶם הֵן

Of Nifal is only found 1. c. pret. נֶהֱלַלְתִּי of which the rest can be formed.

FUTURE.

תְּהַלֵּל יְהַלֵּל
תְּהַלֵּל 2.
אֲהַלֵּל
נְהַלֵּל
יְהַלְלוּ
תְּהַלֵּלְנָה תְּהַלְלוּ
נְהַלֵּל

PARTICIPLE ACTIVE.

מְהַלֵּל { אֲנִי אֵת הוּא

מְהַלְלֵי { מְהַלְלִים אֶם הֵן

The meaning of Piel is the same as in Kal; it is only used in poetry.

FUTURE. *

[תִּתְהַלֵּל] תִּתְהַלֵּל [יִתְהַלֵּל] יִתְהַלֵּל
[תִּתְהַלֵּל] תִּתְהַלֵּל 2.
[אֶתְהַלֵּל] אֶתְהַלֵּל
נִתְהַלֵּל
יִתְהַלְלוּ [יִתְהַלְלוּ]
תִּתְהַלֵּלְנָה [תִּתְהַלְלוּ]
[נִתְהַלֵּל] נִתְהַלֵּל

PARTICIPLE ACTIVE.

מִתְהַלֵּל { אֲנִי אֵת הוּא

מִתְהַלְלֵי { מִתְהַלְלִים אֶם הֵן

Hithpael regular. Pret. הִתְהַלֵּל.
Fut. יִתְהַלֵּל, Particip. מִתְהַלֵּל.

* Those in brackets [ ] are fut. e apocop.

TABLE XII.—IRREGULAR VERB לָקַח to take.

	KAL.		NIFAL.		PUAL.	
	PRETERIT.		**PRETERIT.**		**PRETERIT.**	
	com.	mas.	com.	mas.	com.	mas.
3. sing.		לָקַח		נִלְקַח		לֻקַּח
fem.		לָקְחָה		נִלְקְחָה		לֻקְּחָה
2.		לָקַחְתָּ		נִלְקַחְתָּ		לֻקַּחְתָּ
fem.		לָקַחַתְּ		נִלְקַחַתְּ		לֻקַּחַתְּ
1.	לָקַחְתִּי		נִלְקַחְתִּי		לֻקַּחְתִּי	
3. pl.	לָקְחוּ		נִלְקְחוּ		לֻקְּחוּ	
2.	לְקַחְתֶּם		נִלְקַחְתֶּם		לֻקַּחְתֶּם	
1.	לָקַחְנוּ		נִלְקַחְנוּ		לֻקַּחְנוּ	

INFINITIVE.

KAL — const. קַחַת   abs. לָקוֹחַ
   הִלָּקַח, לָקְחָה, לָקְחָה, לָקַחְתּ

NIFAL — INFINITIVE.
   הִלָּקֵחַ, הִלָּקְחָה, הִלָּקַח, הִלָּקֵחַ
   לְהִלָּקֵחַ, לְהִלָּקַח

PUAL — INFINITIVE.   לֻקַּח

IMPERATIVE.

KAL
   קַח   קְחִי
   לְקָחִי   לְקַח
   קְחוּ   קַחְנָה

NIFAL
   הִלָּקַח   הִלָּקְחִי
   הִלָּקְחוּ   הִלָּקַחְנָה

PUAL — **No Imperative.**

Kal (right column)

Future.

3. sing.	יִקַּח	תִּקַּח
2.	תִּקַּח	תִּקְחִי
1.	אֶקַּח	
3. pl.	יִקְחוּ	תִּקַּחְנָה
2.	תִּקְחוּ	תִּקַּחְנָה
1.	נִקַּח	

Participle Active.

	Masc.	Fem.
1.	אָנֹכִי } לֹקֵחַ	אָנֹכִי } לֹקַחַת
2.	אַתָּה	אַתְּ
3.	הוּא	הִיא
1.	אֲנַחְנוּ } לֹקְחִים	אֲנַחְנוּ } לֹקְחוֹת
2.	אַתֶּם	אַתֶּן
3.	הֵם	הֵן

Participle Passive.

אָנֹכִי לָקוּחַ   אָנֹכִי לְקוּחָה

etc.

אֲנַחְנוּ לְקוּחִים   אֲנַחְנוּ לְקוּחוֹת

etc.

Niphal (middle column)

Future.

3. sing.	יִלָּקַח	תִּלָּקַח
2.	תִּלָּקַח	תִּלָּקְחִי
1.	אֶלָּקַח	
3. pl.	יִלָּקְחוּ	תִּלָּקַחְנָה
2.	תִּלָּקְחוּ	תִּלָּקַחְנָה
1.	נִלָּקַח	

Participle Active.

	Masc.	Fem.
1.	אָנֹכִי } נִלְקָח	אָנֹכִי } נִלְקָחָה
2.	אַתָּה	אַתְּ
3.	הוּא	הִיא
1.	אֲנַחְנוּ } נִלְקָחִים	אֲנַחְנוּ } נִלְקָחוֹת
2.	אַתֶּם	אַתֶּן
3.	הֵם	הֵן

Future.

Is formed from Hofal.

יֻקַּח	תֻּקַּח
תֻּקַּח	תֻּקְּחִי
אֻקַּח	
יֻקְּחוּ	תֻּקַּחְנָה
תֻּקְּחוּ	תֻּקַּחְנָה
נֻקַּח	

Participle Pual.

Masc.	Fem.
אָנֹכִי } לֻקָּח	אָנֹכִי } לֻקָּחָה
אַתָּה	אַתְּ
הוּא	הִיא
אֲנַחְנוּ } לֻקָּחִים	אֲנַחְנוּ } לֻקָּחוֹת
אַתֶּם	אַתֶּן
הֵם	הֵן

Hithpael הִתְלַקַּח, Future יִתְלַקַּח,

Participle מִתְלַקֵּחַ, מִתְלַקַּחַת,

a fire taking hold of itself.

TAB. XIII.— Verb פ"ן and א"ל.

VERB פ"ן and ה"ל.

KAL. (right section)

PRETERIT.

	com. mas.		fem.
3. sing	נָטָה		נָטְתָה
2.	נָטִיתָ		נָטִית
1.	נָטִיתִי		
3. pl.	נָטוּ		
2.	נְטִיתֶם		נְטִיתֶן
1.	נָטִינוּ		

INFINITIVE.

constr. נְטוֹת   abs. נָטוֹ

Imperative: נְטֵה, נְטוֹת, נְטוּ, נְטֶינָה

IMPERATIVE.

נְטֵה   נְטִי

PARTICIPLE PASSIVE.

mas.	fem.
נֹטֶה	נֹטָה

NIFAL.

Pret. נִטָּה, to be stretched out, to elongate itself.

Infinit. absolut. נִטֹּה.
   " const. נִטּוֹת.

Imperative נִטָּה.

KAL. (left section)

PRETERIT.

fem.		com. mas.
יָצְאָה		יָצָא
יָצָאת		יָצָאתָ
		יָצָאתִי
		יָצְאוּ
יְצָאתֶן		יְצָאתֶם
		יָצָאנוּ

INFINITIVE.

const. צֵאת   absol. יָצֹא

Imperative: צֵאת, צֵאתְךָ, צֵאתְכֶם, צֵאתָם

IMPERATIVE.

fem.	mas.
צְאִי	צֵא
צֶאנָה	צְאוּ

75

FUTURE. *

fem.	com.	mas.	
[תִּפֶן] תִּפְנֶה	[יִפֶן] יִפְנֶה	יִפְנֶה	3. sing.
תִּפְנֶה	[תִּפֶן] תִּפְנֶה	תִּפְנֶה	2.
	אֶפְנֶה		1.
תִּפְנֶינָה	יִפְנוּ	יִפְנוּ	3. pl.
תִּפְנֶינָה	תִּפְנוּ	תִּפְנוּ	2.
	[נִפֶן] נִפְנֶה		1.

PARTICIPLE ACTIVE.

פֹּנֶה { פֹּנָה פֹּנֶה אֶת פֹּנֶה לֹּנֶה } פֹּנִי 1. sing.
פֹּנֶה 2.
הוּא 1.

פֹּנוֹת { פֹּנוֹת פֹּנִים אֶת פֹּנָה } פֹּנוּהֶן 3. pl.
אַתֶּם 2.
הֵם 1.

* Those in brackets [ ] are future apocap.

Future תִּפְנֶה.

Participle פֹּנֶה.

Piel and Pual are not used.

HIPHIL.

Pret. הִפְנָה.

Infin. absol. הַפְנֵה.

" construct. הַפְנוֹת

Future יַפְנֶה, apoc. יֶפֶן.

Participle מַפְנֶה, turning aside.

FUTURE.

fem.	com.	mas.	
תֵּצֵא		יֵצֵא	3. sing.
תֵּצֵא		תֵּצֵא	2.
	אֵצֵא		1.
תֵּצֶאנָה		יֵצְאוּ	3. pl.
תֵּצֶאנָה		תֵּצְאוּ	2.
	נֵצֵא		1.

PARTICIPLE ACTIVE.

יוֹצֵא { יֹצְאָה יֹצֵא אֶת יֹצֵא הוּא } יֹצֵא

יוֹצְאוֹת { יוֹצְאוֹת יֹצְאִים אֶת יֹצְאָה הֵן } יֹצְאֵיהֶן

Being an intransitive verb, it has
no participle passive.

TABLE XIV.—VERB פ״י and ל״ה. VERB פ״י and ל״א.

HIFIL.			KAL			HIFIL.			
PRETERIT.			**PRETERIT.**			**PRETERIT.**			
fem.	com.	mas.	fem.	com.	mas.	fem.	com.	mas.	
הוֹרְתָה		הוֹרָה	יָרְתָה		יָרָה	הוֹצִיאָה		הוֹצִיא	3. sing.
הוֹרֵית		הוֹרֵיתָ	יָרֵית		יָרֵיתָ	הוֹצֵאת		הוֹצֵאתָ	2.
	הוֹרֵיתִי			יָרֵיתִי			הוֹצֵאתִי		1.
	הוֹרוּ			יָרוּ			הוֹצִיאוּ		3. pl.
הוֹרֵיתֶן		הוֹרֵיתֶם	יָרֵיתֶן		יָרֵיתֶם	הוֹצֵאתֶן		הוֹצֵאתֶם	2.
	הוֹרֵינוּ			יָרֵינוּ			הוֹצֵאנוּ		1.

INFINITIVE.

KAL: const. יָרוֹת absol. יָרֹה

בִּירוֹת, כִּירוֹת, לִירוֹת, מִירוֹת

HIFIL (פ״י and ל״ה): הוֹרוֹת, בְּהוֹרוֹת, כְּהוֹרוֹת, לְהוֹרוֹת, מֵהוֹרוֹת

HIFIL (פ״י and ל״א): const. הוֹצֵיא absol. הוֹצֵא

כְּהוֹצִיא, לְהוֹצִיא, מֵהוֹצִיא

IMPERATIVE.

HIFIL		KAL		HIFIL	
הוֹרִי	הוֹרֵה	יְרִי	יְרֵה	הוֹצִיאִי	הוֹצֵא
הוֹרֵינָה	הוֹרוּ	יְרֶינָה	יְרוּ	הוֹצֶאנָה	הוֹצִיאוּ

FUTURE.		
[יֵהוֹם] יֵהוֹם [יֵהֹם] יֵהֹם	3. s.
יֵהֹם [יֵהֹם] יֵהֹם	2.
[יֵהֹם] אֵהֹם	1.
יֵהֹמוּ	[יַהֹמוּ] 3. pl.
תֵּהֹמֶינָה	2.
[יֵהֹם] נֵהֹם	1.

PARTICIPLE ACTIVE.

FUTURE.

יֵהֶד	[יֵהֶד]
יֵהֶד	
אֵהֶד	
יֵהֶדוּ	
תֵּהֶדְנָה	
תֵּהֶדְנָה	
נֵהֶד	

PARTICIPLE ACTIVE.

הֹדֶה etc.

PARTICIPLE PASSIVE.

etc.

FUTURE.

יֵקֹם [יֵקֹם]	[יֵקֹם] יֵקֹם
תֵּקֹם	[תֵּקֹם] תֵּקֹם
אָקֹם [אָקוֹם]	
יָקֹמוּ	
תֵּקֹמֶינָה	[יָקֹמוּ]
תֵּקֹמֶינָה	
נֵקֹם [נֵקֹם]	

PARTICIPLE ACTIVE.

קָם etc.

Of Niphal there is found only the Future, יִקֹּם (Ex. xix. 13.).

Those in brackets [ ] are the Future Apocop.

HOPHAL.

Preterit הוּקַם, Future יוּקַם, Participle מוּקָם.

TABLE XV.—VERB פ"נ *and* ל"א.

KAL.

PRETERIT.

	com.	mas.	fem.
3. sing.		נָשָׂא	נָשְׂאָה
2.		נָשָׂאתָ	נָשָׂאת
1.	נָשָׂאתִי		
3. pl.	נָשְׂאוּ		
2.		נְשָׂאתֶם	נְשָׂאתֶן
1.	נָשָׂאנוּ		

INFINITIVE.

abs. נָשׂא

const. שְׂאֵת , לָשֵׂאת , בְּשֵׂאת , כְּשֵׂאת; מִשֵּׂאת

PARTICIPLE ACTIVE.

fem.	mas.	
נֹשֵׂאת {	נֹשֵׂא { אֲנִי 1.	
	אַתָּה 2.	
	הוּא 3.	
נֹשׂאוֹת	נֹשְׂאִים { אֲנַחְנוּ 1.	
	אַתֶּם 2.	
	הֵם 3.	

PARTICIPLE PASSIVE.

fem.	mas.	
נְשׂוּאָה {	נָשׂוּא { אֲנִי 1.	
	אַתָּה 2.	
	הוּא 3.	
נְשׂוּאוֹת	נְשׂוּאִים { אֲנַחְנוּ 1.	
	אַתֶּם 2.	
	הֵם 3.	

PUAL.

Not to be found.

HIFIL.

Pret. הִנְשִׂיא, to bear punishment of his sin.

HITHPAEL.

Pret. הִנַּשֵׂא and הִתְנַשֵּׂא.

All the rest of the Verb is regular.

IMPERATIVE.

| | 2. sing. | שָׂא |
| | 2. pl. | שְׂאוּ |

FUTURE.

	masc.	com.	fem.
3. sing.	יִשָׂא		תִּשָׂא
2.	תִּשָׂא		תִּשָׂא
1.		אֶשָׂא	
3. pl.	יִשְׂאוּ		תִּשֶׂאנָה
2.	תִּשְׂאוּ		תִּשֶׂאנָה
1.		נִשָׂא	

NIFAL.

Pret. נִשָׂא, to lift up one's self.

Infin. absol. נִשָׂאֹה

,, const. נִשָׂאֹה

Imperative נִשָׂאֹה

Future נִשָׂא

Participle נִשָׂא

PIEL.

Pret. נִשֵׂא, to exalt, to help.

Infinitive, נַשֵׂא,

Imperative, idem.

Future נַשֵׂא

Participle מְנַשֵׂא

TABLE XVI.—VERB עו and ל״א.

	HOFAL.	HIFIL.	KAL.

KAL.

PRETERIT.

	com.	mas.	
3. sing. mas.			הֵקִיא
2.			הֲקִאֹתָ
1.	הֲקִאֹתִי		
3. pl.		נֵקִיאוּ	
2.		הֲקֵאתֶם	
1.	הֲקֵאנוּ		

	fem.
	הֵקִיאָה
	הֲקֵאתְ
	(הֲקֶאןָ)

INFINITIVE.

הָקֵא, הָקִיא, הֲקֵאָה, הָקִיאָה, הָקֵא

IMPERATIVE.

הָקֵא
הֲקִיאִי
הֲקִיאוּ
הֲקֶאנָה

HIFIL.

PRETERIT.

	com.	mas.	fem.

INFINITIVE.

IMPERATIVE.

HOFAL.

PRETERIT.

	com.	mas.	fem.

INFINITIVE.

No Imperative.

FUTURE.

			3. sing.
			2.
			1.
			3 pl.
			2.
			1.

PARTICIPLE ACTIVE.

	1.
	2.
	3.

	1.
	2.
	3.

There is no Participle Passive.

FUTURE.

PARTICIPLE ACTIVE.

[‑] in brackets Fut. apoc.

FUTURE.

PARTICIPLE ACTIVE.

TABLE XVII.—VERB לֹ״ה WITH SUFFIXES.

SINGULAR.

PLURAL.

	1. c.	2. m.	2. f.	3. m.	3. f.	1. c.	2. m.	2. f.	3. m.	3. f.
3. m.										
3. f.										
2. m.										
2. f.										
1. c.										
3. pl.										
2. "										
1. "										
Inf.										
Imp.										

Fut.	PARTICIPLE ACTIVE.				PARTICIPLE PASSIVE.			
	sin. mas.	sin. fem.	pl. mas.	pl. fem.	sin. mas.	sin. fem.	pl. mas.	pl. fem.

TABLE XVIII.—VERB ע״ו WITH SUFFIXES.

	PLURAL.					SINGULAR.				
3. fem.	3. masc.	2. fem.	2. masc.	1. com.	3. fem.	3. masc.	2. fem.	2. masc.	1. com.	
שָׂמָן	שָׂמָם	שָׂמְכֶן	שָׂמְכֶם	שָׂמָנוּ	שָׂמָהּ	שָׂמוֹ שָׂמָהוּ	שָׂמֵךְ	שָׂמְךָ	שָׂמַנִי	3. m.
שָׂמָתַן	שָׂמָתַם	שָׂמַתְכֶן	שָׂמַתְכֶם	שָׂמַתָנוּ	שָׂמָתָה	שָׂמַתּוּ שָׂמַתְהוּ	שָׂמָתֵךְ	שָׂמָתְךָ	שָׂמַתְנִי	3. f.
שָׂמְתָּן	שַׂמְתָּם	—	—	שַׂמְתָּנוּ	שְׂמְתָּהּ	שַׂמְתּוֹ שַׂמְתָּהוּ	—	—	שַׂמְתַּנִי	2. m.
שַׂמְתִּין	שַׂמְתִּים	—	—	שַׂמְתִּינוּ	שַׂמְתִּיהָ	שַׂמְתִּיו	—	—	שַׂמְתִּינִי	2. f.
שְׂמְתִּין	שְׂמְתִּים	שַׂמְתִּיכֶן	שַׂמְתִּיכֶם	—	שַׂמְתִּיהָ	שַׂמְתִּיו שְׂמְתִּיהוּ	שַׂמְתִּיךְ	שַׂמְתִּיךָ	—	1. c.

Fut.										
Imp.										
Inf.										
1. c.										
2. c.										
3. c. p.										

TABLE XIX.—VERB DOUBLE ע WITH SUFFIXES.

	PLURAL					SINGULAR				
3. fem.	3. masc.	2. fem.	2. masc.	1. com.	3. fem.	3. masc.	2. fem.	2. mas.	1. com.	
סַבָּן	סַבָּם	סַבְּכֶן	סַבְּכֶם	סַבָּנוּ	סַבָּהּ	סַבּוֹ סַבָּהוּ	סַבֵּךְ	סַבְּךָ	סַבַּנִי	3. m.
סַבָּתָן	סַבָּתָם	סַבַּתְכֶן	סַבַּתְכֶם	סַבַּתְנוּ	סַבַּתָּהּ	סַבַּתְהוּ	סַבַּתֵךְ	סַבַּתְךָ	סַבַּתְנִי	3. f.
סַבֹּתָן	סַבֹּתָם	—	—	סַבֹּתָנוּ	סַבֹּתָהּ	סַבֹּתוֹ	—	—	סַבֹּתַנִי	2. m.
סַבֹּתִים	סַבֹּתָם	—	—	סַבֹּתָנוּ	סַבֹּתִיהָ	סַבֹּתִיו	—	—	סַבֹּתִינִי	2. f.
idem	idem	סַבּוֹתִיכֶן	סַבּוֹתִיכֶם		idem	idem	סַבּוֹתִיךְ	סַבּוֹתִיךְ	—	1. c.
סַבּוּן	סַבּוּם	סַבּוּכֶן	סַבּוּכֶם	סַבּוּנוּ	סַבּוּהָ	סַבּוּהוּ	סַבּוּךְ	סַבּוּךְ	סַבּוּנִי	3. c.
סַבּוֹתִים	סַבּוֹתִים	—	—	סַבּוֹתוּנוּ	סַבּוֹתוּהָ	סַבּוֹתוּהוּ	—	—	סַבּוֹתוּנִי	2. c.
סַבּוֹנוּן	סַבּוֹנוּם	סַבּוֹנוּכֶן	סַבּוֹנוּכֶם	—	סַבּוֹנוּהָ	סַבּוֹנוּהוּ	סַבּוֹנוּךְ	סַבּוֹנוּךְ	—	1. c.
סָבְּכֶן	סָבְּכֶם	סָבְּכֶן	סָבְּכֶם	סָבֵּנוּ	סָבָּהּ	סָבּוֹ	סָבֵּךְ	סָבְּךָ	סָבֵּי	Inf.
סָבֵּן	סָבֵּם	סָבֵּן	—	סָבֵּנוּ	סָבֵּהָ	סָבֵּהוּ	—	—	סָבֵּנִי	Imp.
סָבּוּן	סָבּוּם	—	—	סָבּוּנוּ	סָבּוּהָ	סָבּוּהוּ	—	—	סָבּוּנִי	
יְסֻבֵּן	יְסֻבֵּם	יְסֻבְּכֶן	יְסֻבְּכֶם	יְסֻבֵּנוּ	יְסֻבָּהּ	יְסֻבְּהוּ	יְסֻבֵּךְ	יְסֻבְּךָ	יְסֻבֵּנִי	Fut.

90

INDEX.

88

.

www.ingramcontent.com/pod-product-compliance
Lightning Source LLC
Chambersburg PA
CBHW020304090426
42735CB00009B/1214

* 9 7 8 3 3 3 7 3 1 6 1 5 0 *